A Tale of Two Cities

A play

Matthew Francis

Adapted from the novel by Charles Dickens

Samuel French — London
New York - Toronto - Hollywood

© 1996 BY MATTHEW FRANCIS

Rights of Performance by Amateurs are controlled by Samuel French Ltd, 52 Fitzroy Street, London W1P 6JR, and they, or their authorized agents, issue licences to amateurs on payment of a fee. **It is an infringement of the Copyright to give any performance or public reading of the play before the fee has been paid and the licence issued.**

The Royalty Fee indicated below is subject to contract and subject to variation at the sole discretion of Samuel French Ltd.

> Basic fee for each and every
>   performance by amateurs   Code M
>   in the British Isles

The Professional Repertory Rights in this play are controlled by SAMUEL FRENCH LTD.

The publication of this play does not imply that it is necessarily available for performance by amateurs or professionals, either in the British Isles or Overseas. Amateurs and professionals considering a production are strongly advised in their own interests to apply to the appropriate agents for consent before starting rehearsals or booking a theatre or hall.

ISBN 0 573 01942 8

Please see page iv for further copyright information

LINCOLNSHIRE
COUNTY COUNCIL
822

A TALE OF TWO CITIES

First performed at the Greenwich Theatre on the 15th of December 1994 with the following cast:

Mr Jarvis Lorry	Bernard Lloyd
Miss Pross	Susan Porrett
Lucie Manette	Eleanor Tremain
Dr Manette	Julian Forsyth
Marquis St Evrémonde	Mark Saban
St Evrémonde	Alexis Denisof
The Peasant Boy	Benedict Sandiford
Mme Defarge	Heather Tobias
Defarge	Iain Mitchell
Old Bailey Judge	Bernard Lloyd
Chief Prosecution Witness	Benedict Sandiford
Sydney Carton	Timothy Walker
Attorney General	Charles Dale
Charles Darnay	Alexis Denisof
John Barsad	Mark Saban
Mr Stryver	Iain Mitchell
Gaspard	Charles Dale
Gabelle	Charles Dale
Seamstress	Eleanor Tremain
Court Attendant	Leighton Vickers

Narrators, Coachmen, Postilions, Citizens, Court Officials, Spectators, Jurors, Witnesses, Prosecutors, Judges, Peasants, Aristocrats, Soldiers, Revolutionaries, Servants, played by members of the company

Directed by Matthew Francis
Designed by Julian McGowan
Music by Mia Soteriou
Lighting by Geraint Pughe
Sound by Steve Huttly and John Leonard
Fights by Malcolm Ranson
Production Assistants Emma Whelan and Jon Lee
Deputy Stage Manager Fiona Redman

COPYRIGHT INFORMATION

(See also page ii)

This play is fully protected under the Copyright Laws of the British Commonwealth of Nations, the United States of America and all countries of the Berne and Universal Copyright Conventions.

All rights including Stage, Motion Picture, Radio, Television, Public Reading, and Translation into Foreign Languages, are strictly reserved.

No part of this publication may lawfully be reproduced in ANY form or by any means—photocopying, typescript, recording (including video-recording), manuscript, electronic, mechanical, or otherwise—or be transmitted or stored in a retrieval system, without prior permission.

Licences for amateur performances are issued subject to the understanding that it shall be made clear in all advertising matter that the audience will witness an amateur performance; that the names of the authors of the plays shall be included on all programmes; and that the integrity of the authors' work will be preserved.

The Royalty Fee is subject to contract and subject to variation at the sole discretion of Samuel French Ltd.

In Theatres or Halls seating Four Hundred or more the fee will be subject to negotiation.

In Territories Overseas the fee quoted above may not apply. A fee will be quoted on application to our local authorized agent, or if there is no such agent, on application to Samuel French Ltd, London.

VIDEO-RECORDING OF AMATEUR PRODUCTIONS

Please note that the copyright laws governing video-recording are extremely complex and that it should not be assumed that any play may be video-recorded for whatever purpose without first obtaining the permission of the appropriate agents. The fact that a play is published by Samuel French Ltd does not indicate that video rights are available or that Samuel French Ltd controls such rights.

CHARACTERS

Mr Lorry
Miss Pross
Lucie Manette
Dr Manette
Boy
Mme Defarge
Defarge
Sydney Carton
Judge: *English Court*
Attorney: *English Court*
John Barsad
Mr Stryver
Charles Darnay
Witness
Gaspard
Coachman
Postilion
Gabelle
Marquis St Evrémonde
St Evremonde: *the Marquis's brother*
Governor
Judge: *French Court*
Prosecutor: *French Court*
Chemist
Gaoler
Seamstress
Narrators, Citizens, Court Officials, Jurors, Peasants, Aristocrats, Soldiers, Revolutionaries

PRODUCTION NOTES

The following notes refer to the Greenwich Theatre production of this adaptation directed by the author.

SETTINGS

At Greenwich Julian McGowan designed a brilliantly versatile multi-level set for the production. This allowed each scene to follow the last fluently and quickly. As Miss Pross waved Lucie and Mr Lorry off on their journey to France in one area of the stage, Mme Defarge would appear at her wine shop in another. Atmospheric lighting and the simplest of devices were employed to complete each stage picture. In the wine shop a counter unfolded from within the set and an Inn sign was pulled across. At Dr Manette's, double doors were opened to reveal the dappled light of a Soho courtyard and a table laid for lunch. Two chairs were pulled round a fire grating in the stage floor as Sydney Carton and Mr Lorry quizzed Barsad the spy.

There are quite a number of stagecoach journeys in the play. Double doors at the centre of our set were built in four sections so that they could open like carriage doors. Circular tables used in a number of scenes were attached at other times on either side of the doors and were able to spin like carriage wheels. When the top half of each door was pushed open, and with the use of a good sound effect, the journeys to and from Paris, and out to the chateau of the Marquis, were vividly staged.

It is imperative that the action of the play moves on at a good pace. This adaptation will not be successful if there are huge scene changes which take forever to accomplish. It would be far better to do without a set and suggest each scene with a few simple props and pieces of furniture which the actors bring on themselves than to sink the play beneath a weight of unwieldy stage effects.

THE GUILLOTINE

The guillotine we used at Greenwich was a clever and effective piece of stage machinery. A number of aristocrats were executed in full view of the audience and the effect was alarmingly realistic. The device should have a blade that drops convincingly and retracts into the block on which it is mounted. The "victim" should put his head into the neck halter, the upper half of which swings down to keep the victim in position. The lower section of the neck halter should be made of a strong foam rubber, painted to look like dark wood but with a slit in it so that when the blade drops and retracts, the actor, who has been kneeling, can fall flat on his stomach, pulling his head down through the slit in the foam rubber. The head then appears to drop directly into the basket, which should be large enough to conceal a false head that the executioner can pick up and flourish. With lots of blood splashing about, this effect works brilliantly after only an hour or two's rehearsal.

MUSIC

Mia Soteriou has composed a powerful and evocative score for this adaptation. The full score is available for the play and terms for its use may be obtained through Rachel Daniels at LONDON MANAGEMENT, 2-4 Noel Street, London W1V 3RB (0171 287 9000). Tapes of the music suitable for use in the production are also available. Mia's music includes a number of themes: for the Marquis, the Defarges and an English theme to introduce the scenes in Soho. These are indicated at points throughout the text.

DOUBLING

At Greenwich we contrived to present the play with ten actors playing nearly forty parts. It would be difficult to do the play with fewer than ten but it would be perfectly possible to present it with many more than that.

The lines of narration that are not ascribed to any particular character in the play should be given to any available member of the company, as determined by the director.

THE END

It would be a great mistake to use the guillotine for the Seamstress and Sydney Carton at the end of the play. The guillotine as described is a wonderful but melodramatic device and the audience's delight is focused on trying to puzzle out how the equipment works. To provoke such a reaction at the end of the play would interfere with the emotional impact of Carton's self-sacrifice.

This adaptation is dedicated to my parents
Ronald and **Dorothy Matthews**
— with love and thanks.

ACT I

Scene 1

The Shoemaker

Darkness. The sound of carriage wheels growing steadily louder. Creaks, rumblings; horses neigh, pant, gallop. At its loudest — a sudden braking. The carriage skids and squeals to silence. In the dark we hear the voices of the company. A great shout

All Recalled to life!

And a single match is struck. It lights ten lanterns in an instant. People are crowding to see a single figure — a man — white-haired, sitting on a low bench. This is Dr Manette. He is making a lady's shoe. Tap tap tap. He has a thin hollow face, tattered clothes, a steadfastly vacant gaze. Oppressed, repetitive movements. Figures in the crowd begin to speak

First Buried how long?
Second (*voicing an opinion*) Almost eighteen years.
Third You had abandoned all hope of being dug out?
Second (*as before*) Long ago.
Fourth You know that you are recalled to life?
Fifth I hope you care to live?
Sixth Shall I show her to you?
Seventh Will you come and see her?
First He can't say.
Fifth He can't speak.
Third He doesn't know!
Second He doesn't know her!
Sixth He doesn't understand!!

The crash of a great door. A thunderous, clanging, deadly sound. It echoes through a great, many-chambered building. An eighth figure, Mr Jarvis Lorry, a gentleman of sixty, cries out

Mr Lorry Gracious creator of day! To be buried alive for eighteen years!

Scene 2

Lucie

The other figures scatter. The Light on the shoemaker goes out. It is immediately replaced by firelight. Distant sounds of the sea. Somewhere — a pipe or a fiddle playing

Miss Pross, a wild-looking woman with a bonnet like a great stilton cheese, red hair and a tight red dress, is facing Mr Lorry. He wears a well-worn brown suit, with an odd little sleek crisp flaxen wig on his head

Miss Pross She's here. I brought her.
Gentleman So soon?
Miss Pross Just this minute.
Gentleman (*nervously*) Expected her at five.
Miss Pross (*impatiently*) Heigh-ho-hum!
Gentleman I beg your pardon?
Miss Pross (*accusingly*) Just like a banker!

And Lucie Manette, a pretty, fair-haired, blue-eyed girl comes into the room. She is bright, alert, eager, on the verge of being alarmed. A beat. Miss Pross shoots a warning look at Mr Lorry, and withdraws

Mr Lorry (*nervously*) Recalled to life?
Lucie Recalled to life.
Mr Lorry (*relieved*) Miss Manette?
Lucie Yes.
Mr Lorry In your adopted country, I presume, I cannot do better than address you as a young English lady …?
Lucie If you please, sir … Mr Lorry?
Mr Lorry Mr Lorry. (*And he bows*)
Lucie Yes.
Mr Lorry Mr *Jarvis* Lorry …
Lucie I received a letter from the bank ——
Mr Lorry Yes indeed. I belong to Tellson's Bank. In London. You are, I know, a ward of Tellson's Bank.
Lucie A letter respecting the small property of my poor father, whom I never saw — so long dead …
Mr Lorry (*involuntarily*) Buried.
Lucie Informing me of some discovery which renders it necessary that I should return to my … that I should go to Paris. And that as I am an orphan and have no friend who could go with me, I should place myself, during the journey, under your protection.

Act I, Scene 2   3

Mr Lorry I should be more than happy to execute the charge.
Lucie Sir, I thank you indeed.
Mr Lorry Miss Manette, I am a man of business. I have a business charge to acquit myself of. In your reception of it, don't heed me any more than if I was a speaking machine. It is very difficult to begin ...
Lucie (*suddenly*) Are you quite a stranger to me?
Mr Lorry (*surprised*) Am I not? (*Recovering after a moment*) Dr Manette ——
Lucie My father ——
Mr Lorry Yes. A gentleman of Beauvais, a scientific gentleman — of great repute in Paris ...

And we hear music. On another part of the stage, a figure comes forward. It is Dr Manette, but younger. He is handsome, with dark hair. Dressed smartly. He speaks to the audience

Dr Manette Alexandre Manette. Physician, native of Beauvais, and afterwards resident in Paris.
Mr Lorry (*to Lucie*) He married ——
Lucie Twenty years ago. An English lady. Yes — I know ...
Dr Manette (*rhapsodic*) My wife, beloved of my heart! My fair young English wife!
Lucie My poor dear mother ...
Mr Lorry His affairs — like the affairs of many other French gentlemen — were entirely in Tellson's hands. Mere business relations, miss; there is no friendship in them, nothing like sentiment. I have no feelings; I am a mere *machine* ... I pass my whole life, miss, in turning an immense pecuniary mangle.
Lucie (*helping him*) Mr Lorry. When my mother died I was left an orphan ... (*deciding to risk it*) and I begin to think it was you who brought me to England. I'm almost sure it was you.
Mr Lorry (*after a moment; happy, relieved*) Miss Manette — it was I.

They grasp hands

(*Resuming*) Yes indeed — your mother. A lady of great courage and spirit, who, when your father disappeared ——
Lucie Disappeared?
Mr Lorry Disappeared, vanished perhaps — the word is not material, either word will do ...
Lucie The word is most material, Mr Lorry. My father died before I knew him ...
Mr Lorry But if your father had not died ... when he did ...
Lucie (*quietly*) You frighten me.

Mr Lorry (*agitated*) Pray, pray control your agitation.
Lucie Oh, I entreat you tell me more ...
Mr Lorry I will. I am going to. You can bear it?
Lucie I can bear anything — anything but the uncertainty you leave me in at this moment.
Dr Manette (*to the audience*) One cloudy moonlight night, in the third week of December, in the year 1757, I was walking in the suburb of Saint Antoine in Paris ...
Mr Lorry If Monsieur Manette had not died. If he had suddenly and silently disappeared ...

SCENE 3

1757

The Light shifts away from Mr Lorry and Lucie but stays on Dr Manette. The suburbs of St Antoine. Shadowy figures

The Citizens group and re-group as the following story is told

Dr Manette The suburb of Saint Antoine in Paris. Samples of a people that had undergone a terrible grinding and re-grinding in the mill, shivered at every corner, passed in and out at every doorway, looked from every window, fluttered in every vestige of a garment that the wind shook.
First Citizen The children had ancient faces and grave voices. And upon them, and upon the grown faces was the sign — HUNGER.
Second Citizen Hunger was pushed out of the tall houses, in the wretched clothing that hung upon poles and lines.
Third Citizen Hunger was patched into them with straw and rag and wood and paper.
First Citizen Hunger stared down from the smokeless chimneys and started up from the filthy streets.
Third Citizen Hunger was the inscription on the baker's shelves, written in every small loaf of his scanty stock of bad bread ——
First Citizen — at the sausage shop, in every dead-dog preparation that was offered for sale.

Dr Manette watches the Citizens. We hear the sound of a carriage approaching

Dr Manette I found myself an hour's distance from my place of residence in the Street of the School of Medicine, when a carriage came along behind me, driven very fast ...

Act I, Scene 3

First Citizen The common people dispersed before the sweating horses, and barely managed to escape from being run down.

A voice inside the carriage cries "Stop!" and two men jump lightly down. Both are muffled. One is the young Marquis St Evrémonde; the second, his brother

Marquis You are Dr Manette?
Dr Manette I am.
Marquis Formerly of Beauvais — an expert surgeon —
Second Man — with a rising reputation in Paris.
Marquis We have been to your residence, and learnt that we might find you here.
Second Man There is a young woman —
Marquis (*cutting him off*) Will you please to enter the carriage?

A moment

Dr Manette Gentlemen, pardon me, but I usually inquire who does me the honour to seek my assistance, and what is the nature of the case to which I am summoned.
Second Man (*impatient*) Your clients are people of condition. As to the nature of the case, you will surely ascertain it for yourself better than we can describe it.
Marquis Enough. The Doctor is persuaded.

The journey

Dr Manette The carriage left the streets behind, passed the north barrier, and emerged upon the country road.
First Citizen In the villages they passed, taxers and taxed were fast asleep.
Second Citizen Dreaming perhaps of banquets, as the starved usually do, the lean inhabitants slept fitfully.
Dr Manette After some hour or seventy minutes we stopped at a great house and turned to a stable building almost hidden by trees.
Marquis This way. Follow quickly.

They enter the stable. There are the sounds of horses moving, rustling straw, soft whinnying. Then the sound of a woman in high fever, gasping for breath, then screaming out: "My husband, my father"

Your patient, Doctor. She has a high fever.
Dr Manette How long has it lasted?

Marquis Since about this hour last night.
Dr Manette I must see her at once.
Marquis Follow me.

They turn to a staircase

A seventeen year-old boy, "a handsome peasant", enters on the stairs and bars their way. He carries an old sword

Boy Stay back. You shall not go to her again!
Marquis Mordieu!
Second Man Who is he?
Marquis A dog. A crazed young dog.
Boy (*defiantly*) Her brother, sir!
Second Man Out of our way.
Boy You shall not go to her!
Second Man How dare you!
Boy Oh you are proud, Monsieur. But we common dogs are proud too sometimes. You plunder us, beat us, kill us; but we have a little pride left — sometimes.
Dr Manette I am a doctor, boy. Let me examine her.
Boy No! I do not want her "examined". Let her be!
First Man Give him money.
Boy You cannot buy me now — when you have robbed us for so long.
Dr Manette It may be I can help the girl ——
Boy She is my sister, Doctor. They have had their shameful rights, these nobles, in the modesty and virtue of our sisters, many years ...
Second Man (*snarling*) Be silent!
Marquis (*calmly*) How — inconvenient. You must teach him a lesson, my brother.
Second Man I would not stain my sword with his blood.
Marquis (*smiling*) You shall have another.
Dr Manette (*protesting*) Gentlemen!
Marquis (*warning*) It is a gentleman's business.

And the Second Man draws his sword and thrusts at the Boy, who makes a spirited if clumsy defence. After an interchange of strokes, the Second Man stumbles, and Dr Manette finds himself between the Boy and his assailant

Boy And how did these two persuade my sister's husband to make her willing?
Marquis The girl's fever is catching, Doctor. Would you prescribe the letting of blood?

Act I, Scene 4   7

Dr Manette By no means ...
Boy They harnessed him to a cart and drove him. They kept him out in the unwholesome mists at night, and ordered him back into his harness in the day. But he was not persuaded. No! Taken out of his harness one day at noon, he sobbed twelve times, once for every stroke of the bell, and died on her bosom ...
Second Man As you shall die now ...
Boy (*passionate*) This brother took her away — for his pleasure and diversion, for a little while. Worn down with grief and suffering, our father's heart burst. My sister fell into a madness ... A victim of this proud, inhuman lord!!
Second Man (*pushing Dr Manette aside*) You cur!

A fierce interchange of blows. Horses neigh and stamp in their stalls. The Boy doesn't stand a chance. The noble blade finds its target — right in the Boy's ribs. He staggers back into Dr Manette's arms. Music — distant, ominous ...

Boy (*to the First Man*) Marquis; in the days when all these things are to be answered for, I summon you and yours — to the last of your bad race — to answer for them. I mark this cross of blood upon you, as a sign that I do it. (*And he puts his fingers to the wound at his breast, and with his forefinger, draws a cross in the air*) Doctor. You are my witness. In the days when all these things are to be answered for. You are my witness ... (*And he falls to the ground*)

An awful silence. From the darkness, voices: "Our witness — you are our witness". The two noblemen stare at Dr Manette. The Lights fade. Music swells up

SCENE 4

The Discovery

The music fades

Firelight again. Mr Lorry and Lucie face one another

Mr Lorry If Monsieur Manette had not died; if he had suddenly and silently disappeared; if his enemies could exercise the privilege of consigning anyone to the oblivion of a prison for any length of time — then you might comprehend the motive and the purpose for our journey today.

Lucie (*faintly*) And my mother?
Mr Lorry She implored the King, the Queen, the court, the clergy, for any tidings of him, but all in vain. At last she came to the determination of sparing her poor child the inheritance of any part of her agony, by rearing her in the belief that her father was dead.
Lucie (*dazed*) I was told of a discovery, sir.
Mr Lorry Ah yes. (*A moment*) He has been — been found. He is alive. Greatly changed, it is too probable. Still, alive. He has been taken to the house of an old servant in Paris, and we are going there ...

Lucie faints

Oh dear! Oh dear dear me! Miss Manette! She doesn't notice a word. This is most confusing. How am I to transact business if I am confused. (*Calling*) Hallo! Hallo there!

The door bursts open and in comes Miss Pross plus two gawping servants

Miss Pross Oh my precious! My bird! (*To the Servants*) Why look at you all! Why don't you go and fetch things instead of standing there staring at me? I'm not so much to look at, am I? I'll let you know, if you don't bring smelling salts, cold water and vinegar, quick, I will.

The Servants flee

Mr Lorry (*to himself*) I really think this must be a man.
Miss Pross (*to Lorry*) And you in brown! Couldn't you tell her what you had to tell her without frightening her to death? Look at her, with her pretty pale face and her cold hands. Do you call that being a banker?!
Mr Lorry (*nonplussed*) I hope she will do well now ...
Miss Pross No thanks to you in brown, if she does.
Mr Lorry I hope that you may accompany Miss Manette to France?
Miss Pross A likely thing too! If it was ever intended that I should go across salt water, do you suppose Providence would have cast my lot in an island?!

The Lights change

Scene 5

The Wine Shop

Travelling music. A shanty. Seagulls. More thundering wheels. During this we hear voices: "Buried how long?"; "Almost 18 years."; "You had

Act I, Scene 5

abandoned all hope of being dug out?"; "Long ago."; "You know that you are recalled to life?"

Then: Paris. The Lights come up on the wine shop belonging to Defarge. A high building. The counter and public bar at the ground floor, then staircases leading up to a hundred filthy little rooms. The first thing we see is Mme Defarge sitting behind the counter, knitting, then figures sitting or standing in the street outside, lastly the figure of Dr Manette in a room near the top of the building. A single pipe plays on, almost keeping a rhythm with the occasional tap tap tap of the shoemaker and the click clack of the knitting needles. Mr Lorry and Miss Manette stand before Mme Defarge

Mr Lorry (*risking the password*) Recalled to life ...?

But there is no response

(*Nervously*) Am I correct in taking this to be the wineshop of Monsieur Defarge?

Mme Defarge knits on, staring at him, and raises an eyebrow. Mr Lorry shifts nervously

Monsieur Defarge expects us. Our business is with him.

She knits on, stares, lifts her eyebrow a shade further

(*In desperation*) You work hard, Madame.
Mme Defarge Yes. (*A long moment*) I have a good deal to do.
Mr Lorry What do you make, Madame?
Mme Defarge Many things.
Mr Lorry For instance ...?
Mme Defarge For instance ... (*another moment*) ... shrouds.

Lucie gasps faintly, Lorry twitches

Defarge steps forward from the darkness. Lorry turns to him. He tries the password again

Mr Lorry Recalled to life?
Defarge (*quickly*) Recalled to life.
Mr Lorry (*immensely relieved*) This is our man!
Defarge (*looking at Lucie closely*) You are his daughter?

Lorry nods. Defarge drops down on one knee in front of Lucie and puts her hand to his lips. Lucie is astonished. Defarge stands

Come this way. It is very high; it is a little difficult; better to begin slowly.

They climb the stairs during the following

Mr Lorry Is he alone?
Defarge Alone! God help him, who should be with him?
Mr Lorry Is he always alone?
Defarge Yes.
Mr Lorry He is greatly changed?
Defarge Changed?! God take their souls to everlasting hell!!

They arrive at the door to Dr Manette's room. Defarge unlocks it, pushes it open. Lucie holds back

Lucie I am afraid of it ...
Mr Lorry Of it? Of what?
Lucie I mean of him. Of my father ...

Mr Lorry puts an encouraging arm around her. They enter the room. A long moment. Dr Manette pauses, doesn't look at them, continues with his work

Defarge Good-day.
Dr Manette (*a faint voice: "the faintness of solitude and disuse"*) Good-day ...
Defarge You are still hard at work, I see.
Dr Manette (*after a moment*) Yes — I am working.
Defarge You have a visitor, you see.
Dr Manette What did you say?
Defarge A visitor. (*A beat*) Come. Here is Monsieur, who knows a well-made shoe when he sees one. Show him that shoe you are working at ...

There is no reaction

Tell Monsieur what kind of shoe it is, and the maker's name.
Dr Manette (*after a beat*) I forget what it was you asked me. What did you say?
Defarge I said: couldn't you describe the kind of shoe, for Monsieur's information?
Dr Manette It is a lady's shoe. It is a young lady's walking shoe. It is in the present mode. I never saw the mode. I have had a pattern in my hand.
Defarge And the maker's name?

Act I, Scene 5   11

Dr Manette makes an uneasy movement. "The task of recalling Manette from the vacancy into which he always sinks when he has spoken is like recalling some very weak person from a swoon"

Dr Manette Did you ask my name?
Defarge Assuredly I did.
Dr Manette One Hundred and Five, North Tower.
Defarge Is that all?
Dr Manette One Hundred and Five, North Tower.

Mr Lorry moves to him, Lucie holds back

Mr Lorry You are not a shoemaker by trade?
Dr Manette (*hesitantly*) I am not a shoemaker by trade? No, I was not a shoemaker by trade. I — I learnt it here. I taught myself. I asked leave to ... (*a long beat*) ... I asked leave to teach myself, and I — got it with much difficulty after a long while, and I have made shoes ever since. (*He looks away, holding the shoe out to Lorry*)
Mr Lorry (*risking*) Dr Manette?

Dr Manette suddenly drops the shoe. A tense moment

Do you remember nothing of me?
Defarge Have you recognized him, Monsieur?
Mr Lorry Yes. For a moment. I have unquestionably seen, for a single moment, the face that I once knew so well. I ——

Lucie moves forward into the room. At first Dr Manette is unaware of her presence. At length he notices the hem of her skirt and looks up. He starts, looks at her again. A fearful gaze

Dr Manette (*in the pauses of his quick and laboured breathing*) What is this? You are not the gaoler's daughter?
Lucie (*very close to tears*) No.
Dr Manette Who are you?

Lucie kneels by Dr Manette.

(*Staring at her; haltingly*) The same. The same hair. How can it be! She had laid her head upon my shoulder, that night — she had a fear of my going ... How was this? Was it you?

Dr Manette suddenly turns and holds Lucie. Defarge and Lorry start forward anxiously

Lucie I entreat you, good gentlemen, do not come near us, do not speak, do not move ...
Dr Manette (*agonized*) Whose voice was that? No, no. You are too young. It can't be. (*A beat*) See what the prisoner is. These are not the hands she knew, this is not the voice she ever heard. No, no. Tell me. What is your name, my gentle angel?

During Lucie's following speech, Dr Manette's agitation subsides, his vacancy changing into the first glimmer of understanding. He begins to weep

Lucie (*softly*) Oh sir, at another time you shall know my name, and who my mother was, and who my father, and how I never knew their hard, hard history. If you hear in my voice — I don't know that it is so, but I hope it is — if you hear in my voice any resemblance to a voice that once was sweet music in your ears, weep for it! If — when I tell you that your agony is over, and that I have come to take you from it — I cause you to think of your useful life laid waste, and of your native France so wicked to you — weep for it, weep for it. And if, when I shall tell you my name, you learn that I have to kneel to my honoured father and implore his pardon for never having striven day and night for his sweet sake — weep for it ... Good gentlemen — thank God! I feel his tears upon my face, and his sobs strike against my heart. Oh, see. Thank God for this, thank God!

Music rises immediately

SCENE 6

The Journey Home

Defarge and Lorry help Dr Manette to his feet, gather his workbench and tools, then hurry down the stairs. Lucie follows at a distance, helping her father

Mr Lorry (*anxiously*) But is he fit for the journey?
Defarge (*impatiently*) More fit than to remain in this city ...
Lucie (*softly*) You remember the place, my father? You remember coming up here?
Dr Manette What did you say? Remember? No. No — I don't remember. It was so very long ago ...

Act I, Scene 6

Defarge and Lorry arrive below; they talk to the audience

Mr Lorry Within two hours, Mr Lorry ——
Defarge —— and Monsieur Defarge ——
Mr Lorry —— had made all ready for the journey, and had brought with them, beside travelling cloaks and wrappers, bread and meat ——
Defarge (*emphatically*) Wine!
Mr Lorry (*reproachfully*) — and hot coffee.

Lucie and Dr Manette arrive below

Mr Lorry On reaching the courtyard they heard him mutter: One Hundred and Five, North Tower ...
Defarge (*to the audience*) And when he looked about him, it evidently was for the strong fortress walls which had long encompassed him.
Mr Lorry No crowd was about the door.

Mme Defarge appears

Mme Defarge Only one soul was to be seen, and that was Madame Defarge — who leaned against the door-post, knitting, and saw nothing.

They clamber into the coach

Defarge To the barrier!

The sound of hooves and wheels

Lucie The coachman cracked his whip, and they clattered away, under a grove of feebler and feebler over-swinging lamps, out under the great grove of stars ——

The sounds of the journey die away. A beat. Silence

The figure of Sydney Carton is discovered, illuminated by a dim street lamp

Carton — beneath that arch of unmoved and eternal lights; some so remote from this little earth that the learned tell us it is doubtful whether their rays have even yet discovered it, as a point in space where anything is suffered or done.

We hear the carriage again, but it disappears from our sight; the sound continues under the following. Voices repeat the questions asked of Dr Manette

First Voice Buried how long?

Then the sound of a gavel beaten on a block. One two three. The sound of a courtroom

Second Voice Almost eighteen years!
Third Voice You had abandoned all hope of being dug out?

The gavel again. One two three!

Second Long ago!
Mr Lorry I hope you care to be recalled to life?

The gavel. BANG BANG BANG!

Dr Manette I can't say ... I can't say ...

SCENE 7

The Old Bailey

A rising tide of voices, chattering and shouting, takes over from the sound of the carriage. We become aware of a Judge, very high up, banging his gavel. He calls to the audience in an irritated manner

Judge Five years later!

Much hustle and bustle as we arrive in his courtroom. Wigs and gowns appear, a scales of justice is dusted down

First Court Person In *England*!

Everyone cheers dutifully

>In England there was scarcely an amount of order or protection to justify much national boasting!

Judge (*petulantly, banging*) *Five years later!*
First Court Person Daring burglaries by armed men, and highway robberies took place in the capital every night.
Second Court Person The highwayman in the dark was a City tradesman in the light, and — being recognized and challenged by his fellow tradesman — gallantly shot him through the head and rode away ...
First Court Person (*much entertained*) That magnificent potentate, the Lord Mayor of London ——

Act I, Scene 7   15

Jeers, boos, the thud of a rotten tomato

— was made to stand and deliver on Turnham Green by one highwayman —
Second Court Person — who despoiled the illustrious creature in sight of all his retinue ...

Laughter

Judge *Five years later!*

A scruffy figure in tattered gown and barrister's wig pushes through the mêlée. It is Sydney Carton. As he speaks, he settles in a negligent way at the barristers' table

Carton The hangman — ever busy, and ever worse than useless — was in constant requisition. Today, taking the life of an atrocious murderer, and tomorrow of a wretched pilferer who had robbed a farmer's boy of sixpence.

Suddenly an assortment of dead bodies drops down on ropes

Judge The Old Bailey!

Another cheer

The Lights come up fully on the court. It is an absurd place. The Judge is very high up, the dead bodies dangle, gawping puppets represent a group of prurient spectators. It is absurd — but threatening. The dock and witness box face one another. In front of the Judge's bench is a great table of papers/briefs/books at which Carton lounges. Next to him, Stryver, a portly figure in wig and gown. At the opposite end, Mr Attorney General and his team. Two morbid spectators (the Second a woman) are above and behind, or out in the audience

Carton The Old Bailey was famous as a kind of deadly inn yard, from which pale travellers set out continually in carts and coaches on a violent passage into the other world.

During the following, the courtroom buzz continues at a lower level and court procedure continues in dumbshow

First Spectator What's on?
Second Spectator Nothing yet.
First Spectator What's coming on?

Second Spectator Charles Darnay.
First Spectator What one's that?
Second Spectator The treason case.
First Spectator The quartering one, eh?
Second Spectator (*with relish*) Ah! He'll be drawn on a hurdle to be half-hanged, and then he'll be taken down and sliced before his own face, and then his inside will be taken out and burnt while he looks on, and then his head will be chopped off, and he'll be cut into quarters. That's the sentence.
First Spectator If he's found guilty, you mean to say?
Second Spectator Oh — they'll find him guilty — don't you be afraid of that ...

And the buzz rises again

Judge Silence in court!

The buzzing dies away

Will the accused, Charles Darnay, stand forward!

And Charles Darnay comes into the dock. A young man of twenty-five, well-grown and well-looking, with a sunburnt cheek and a dark eye. Pale but calm

The court strains to look at Darnay. The buzz rises again

Judge Charles Darnay! You stand accused as a false traitor to our Lord the King, by reason of your having on divers occasions and by divers ways and means, assisted Louis the French King, by wickedly, falsely and traitorously revealing to the said French Louis what forces our Lord the King had in preparation to send to Canada and North America for the punishment and subjugation of his rebellious, disobedient and insolent subjects there. *How do you plead?*
Darnay Not guilty!
Judge Mr Attorney General?

The grand figure rises to his feet and addresses the jury

Attorney M'lord, gentlemen of the jury: the prisoner before you, though young in years, is old in the treasonable practices which claim the forfeit of his life. The prisoner has, for many years, been in the habit of passing and re-passing between France and England on secret business of which

Act I, Scene 7

he can give no honest account. It is a happy circumstance that Providence has put it into the heart of a shining citizen, formerly the prisoner's friend, to ferret out the nature of the prisoner's schemes, and, struck with horror, to disclose them to His Majesty's Chief Secretary of State. I call Mr John Barsad.

Buzz buzz buzz. Cries of "John Barsad", "Call Mr John Barsad!"

And he pops up

You are?
Barsad Mr John Barsad.
Attorney A gentleman?
Barsad Yes!
Attorney And Patriot?
Barsad All my life.
Attorney Are you acquainted with the prisoner?
Barsad These five years.
Attorney D'you know him well?
Barsad Very well.
Attorney How well?
Barsad Day and night. Hardly out of his company.
Attorney Very well.
Barsad Very well.
Attorney Do you see these lists?
Barsad Very clearly.
Attorney Do you recognize these lists?
Barsad Very much so.
Attorney Lists of His Majesty's forces.
Barsad Of their disposition and preparation ——
Attorney Both by land and sea. Where have you seen these lists?
Barsad In the prisoner's pockets.
Attorney And?
Barsad In the prisoner's desk.
Attorney *And?*
Barsad *(with a flourish)* In the prisoner's hands when he spoke to gentlemen!
Attorney *French* gentlemen ...
Barsad Both at Calais and Boulogne.
Attorney When was this?
Barsad Many times.
Attorney But the first time?

Barsad Five years ago, within a few weeks ——
Attorney (*not waiting for the information*) — within a few weeks of the very first action fought between the British troops and the Americans!!

Buzz buzz. Big sensation. Mr Attorney General concludes his cross-examination

    No further questions!
Judge Mr Stryver!

The buzz dies away, as Stryver gets slowly to his feet

Stryver Have you ever been a spy yourself?
Barsad No! I scorn the base insinuation! I ——
Stryver What d'you live on?
Barsad Property.
Stryver Where is it?
Barsad I can't recall precisely where it is. I ——
Stryver What is it?
Barsad That's no business of anybody's ——
Stryver Inherit it?
Barsad Yes ——
Stryver From whom?
Barsad Relations.
Stryver Distant?
Barsad Distant.
Stryver Very distant?
Barsad Very distant.
Stryver Ever been in prison?
Barsad No and no again!
Stryver Debtors' prison?
Barsad Well I ——
Stryver Never?
Barsad Yes.
Stryver How many times?
Barsad Two or three times.
Stryver Not five or six?
Barsad Perhaps.
Stryver And your profession?
Barsad I am a gentleman!
Stryver Ever been kicked?
Barsad Well ——
Stryver Frequently?
Barsad No!

Act I, Scene 7   19

Stryver Ever been kicked downstairs?
Barsad Certainly not!
Stryver No?
Barsad Once received a kick at the top of a staircase, and fell downstairs — quite of my own accord.
Stryver Kicked on that occasion for cheating at dice?
Barsad That was a slander by the drunken liar who committed the assault, but —
Stryver D'you ever borrow money of the prisoner?
Barsad Yes ...
Stryver Ever pay him?
Barsad No ...
Stryver Is not your intimacy with the prisoner in reality a very slight one — forced upon the prisoner in coaches, inns and packets ...?
Barsad No!
Stryver Are you certain that you saw the prisoner with these lists?
Barsad Yes!
Stryver You had no prior knowledge of the lists?
Barsad No!
Stryver Or procured these lists yourself for instance?
Barsad *No!*
Stryver Or expect to get anything by this evidence?!
Barsad NO!
Stryver Not in regular government pay and employment to lay traps?
Barsad Certainly not!
Stryver You swear that?!
Barsad No! — that is — Yes!!

Loud buzzing. Barsad, the Judge and the Attorney General gesticulate at one another wordlessly

Judge (*above the buzz*) Call Miss Lucie Manette.

Voices: "Miss Manette, Miss Lucie Manette" etc. Buzz buzz

   She appears. She stands, seemingly uncertain

   Dr Manette rises and helps Lucie to climb into the witness box

First Spectator Who's this?
Second Spectator Witness.
First Spectator And who's the gent?
Second Spectator Her father.

First Spectator Who's called her?
Second Spectator The prosecution.
First Spectator Against the prisoner?
Second Spectator Against the prisoner.

Lucie and Darnay face one another. Buzz buzz

Attorney Miss Manette: you have seen the prisoner before?
Lucie Yes, sir.
Attorney Where?
Lucie I was returning from France five years ago. At Calais, the prisoner came on board ...
Attorney At what hour did he come on board?
Lucie At a little after midnight ...
Attorney (*grimly*) In the dead of night.

A big reaction from the court

Had he come on board alone?
Lucie No.
Attorney How many were with him?
Lucie Two French gentlemen ...
Attorney Had any papers been handed about among them, similar to these lists?
Lucie Some papers had been handed about among them ...
Attorney Like these in shape and size?
Lucie Possibly, but the light was very dim.
Attorney Now, to the prisoner's conversation, Miss Manette.
Lucie (*fervently, looking across at Darnay*) The prisoner was as open in his confidence with me as he was kind and good and useful to my father. I hope I may not repay him by doing him any harm today.
Attorney *Please go on.*
Lucie He told me he was travelling on business of a delicate and difficult nature which might get people into trouble, and that he was therefore travelling under an assumed name. He said that this business might take him backwards and forwards between France and England for a long time to come.
Attorney Did he say anything about America, Miss Manette? Be particular.
Lucie He explained to me how the quarrel had arisen, and he said that so far as he could judge — it was a wrong and foolish one on England's part. He added ...
Attorney Yes?

Act I, Scene 7   21

The court freezes, staring at Lucie, who looks across at Darnay, remembering

Darnay I think it not unlikely, Miss Manette — that George Washington might gain almost as great a name in history as George III ...

An outburst of laughter and splutter from the blue-flies

Lucie (*protesting*) But there was no harm in his way of saying this: it was said laughingly, and to beguile the time ...
Attorney (*pleased*) Thank you Miss Manette. That will be all.
Lucie But I ——
Attorney That will be *all*.

And Dr Manette helps her down. Buzz buzz

Judge (*to the audience*) A singular circumstance then arose in the case.
Attorney (*irritated*) The prosecution had called a witness to identify the prisoner as having been — at a particular time — in the coffee-room of the *Duke's Head* in a garrison-and-dockyard town.
Witness It was most certainly the prisoner!
Attorney When the prisoner's junior counsel ——
Stryver — my learned friend ——
Judge — whose careless, slovenly appearance bespoke a life disreputable if not quite debauched! ——
Attorney — rose to his feet ...
Second Spectator (*to her friend*) I'd hold half a guinea that he don't get no law work to do. Don't look like the sort of one to get any, do he ...?

Carton saunters in the direction of the witness box. The court falls very silent

Carton You are quite sure it was the prisoner?
Witness Quite sure.
Carton D'you ever see anybody very like the prisoner?
Witness (*confidently*) Not so like that I could be mistaken.
Carton Not so like as me? (*He takes off his wig*)

There are gasps of astonishment. Carton turns so that he and Darnay can be compared. A "moment". Every eye is riveted on them. Maybe a sigh is audible, or an echo of some distant music

Witness Well — I ...
First Spectator Like his twin!
Second Spectator Bust me!

Attorney A certain likeness ...
Judge Remarkable.
Witness But I ——
Carton Perhaps we've met before. I like the *Duke's Head* — though not the coffee-room ...
Judge Are we to try you for treason, Mr Carton?
Carton If your Lordship pleases ... (*And he slopes back to his seat, jams his wig on, and resumes his contemplation of the middle distance*)
Stryver (*leaping to his feet; to the Witness*) Are you still so certain it was the prisoner you saw?
Witness Well yes ...
Stryver Even when you see, by chance, another man so very like him?
Witness I — er ...
Stryver Say how the man you saw was like the prisoner rather than my learned friend?
Witness Um ... er ...
Stryver Perhaps it was another man you saw?
Witness Well ...
Stryver If, that is, you saw a man at all and we are not to find in your testimony the vile and infamous character of evidence too often disfiguring such cases as these, and of which the state trials of this country, gentlemen of the jury, are all too full!
Judge Mr Stryver! Mr Stryver! I cannot sit upon the bench and suffer these allusions. I shall find you in contempt, I shall find you in contempt!!

And the buzz and mutter rise again. It carries through now until the jury retires. We catch phrases and snatches of Stryver amidst the noise

Stryver ... the "patriot" Barsad is nothing more than a hired spy, and a traitor himself ... an unblushing trafficker in blood — a Judas ...

Buzz buzz

> ... the eyes of this spy rested upon the prisoner as a victim, because some family affairs in France required his making those passages across the channel ...

Buzz buzz

> ... evidence warped and wrested from the young lady has come to nothing ...

Buzz buzz

Act I, Scene 7

... the prisoner to be a loyal friend of this glorious country, an ally of our gracious Lord the King, and wholly innocent of the intolerable lies and fictions fabricated by the prosecution!

Buzz buzz. Bang bang bang. Noise and dispute

Judge The jury will withdraw to consider their verdict.

The jury are out in the audience. All eyes on stage turn out to them. Silence. We hear a clock ticking. The tension is too much for Lucie, who nearly faints

Carton Officer! Look to that young lady. Help her father to take her out. Don't you see that she will fall ...

And Lucie is helped to the door by her father and a court official

Tick tick tick. The Lights change. The Judge dozes, others sit, sprawl, read

Darnay An hour and a half limped heavily away ...

Carton moves to Darnay

Carton Mr Darnay! You will naturally be anxious to hear of the witness, Miss Manette. She will do very well. You have seen the worst of her agitation.
Darnay I am deeply sorry to have been the cause of it.
Carton What do you expect, Mr Darnay?
Darnay The worst.
Carton It is the wisest thing to expect, and the likeliest. But I think their long deliberation is in your favour.

And suddenly, startlingly — the gavel again. Bang bang bang. Everyone sits up, stands, stares out at the audience again

Judge Gentlemen of the Jury — how do you find the prisoner?
Voice *(after a long moment, from the audience)* NOT GUILTY!!

And the buzzing swells for the last time — but in amongst it are cheers and shouts, expressions of disbelief from the Attorney General, irritation from the Judge, delight from Stryver and so on

A burst of joyful music

Scene 8

Celebration

The courtroom melts away and two waiters (perhaps) build the basics of an inn around the celebrating party. This is: Lucie, Dr Manette, Stryver, Darnay and, slightly apart, Carton. Snatches of their conversation cover our arrival here. By the end of this sequence they have glasses of wine and are standing in a group

Dr Manette Our congratulations ...
Lucie ... our relief and joy at this conclusion ...
Stryver ... a wholly satisfactory outcome ...
Lucie You may hardly comprehend my anxiety that the evidence which I had given ...
Darnay My grateful thanks to all ...
Stryver ... a success, an indisputable success ...
Darnay ... there are no words to express ...

... and so on

Stryver I am glad to have brought you off with honour, Mr Darnay. It was an infamous prosecution, grossly infamous, but not the less likely to succeed on that account.
Darnay You have laid me under an obligation to you for life.
Stryver I have done my best for you Mr Darnay, and my best is as good as another man's, I believe.
Lucie (*hastily, because nobody else has said it*) Much better!
Stryver You think so? Well! You have been present all day, and ought to know ...
Lucie Mr Darnay ... you look pale ...
Darnay I hardly seem yet to belong to this world again.
Lucie Mr Darnay, my father is anxious to thank you for your kindness to him five years ago.
Darnay You are much recovered, sir, for which we should all give thanks.

Dr Manette comes forward to shake Darnay's hand. As he does so, he stares at the younger man's face, and turning pale, recoils from him. Stryver and Lucie leap forward to support him. Maybe we hear the voice of the Peasant Boy: "In the days when all things are to be answered for — you are my witness ..."

Dr Manette (*to himself*) I must be about my work. I've been too idle ... a lady's shoe ...

Act I, Scene 8   25

Lucie (*alarmed*) Father, Father!
Dr Manette (*rallying*) Forgive me, forgive me. Such a day. I am a little faint.
Lucie Shall we go home?
Dr Manette Yes, yes. It would be best. (*A moment*) Mr ... Darnay. My congratulations to you ...
Lucie Good-night Mr Darnay. I hope we may see you again.
Darnay (*warmly*) A hope I most fervently share ...
Lucie Mr Stryver — will you see us to a carriage? We are all in need of sleep.
Stryver Speak for yourself, Miss Manette, speak for yourself. I have a night's work to do yet. (*He turns to Carton*) Memory! I shall see you at ten. Tonight at ten. Good-night Mr Darnay, good-night, good-night ... Come along, come along ...

And he sweeps Lucie and her father away before him. Darnay stares after them

Carton (*from the shadows*) Do you feel yet that you belong to this terrestrial scheme again, Mr Darnay?
Darnay I — I am still confused regarding time and place ... but I am so far mended as to feel that.
Carton (*bitterly*) It must be an immense satisfaction! (*He fills his glass*) As to me, the greatest desire I have is to forget that I belong to it. It has no good in it for me — except wine like this — nor I for it. So we are not much alike in that particular, nor any particular, you and I ...

An awkward silence

Why don't you call a health, Mr Darnay; why don't you give your toast?
Darnay What health? What toast?
Carton Why — it's on the tip of your tongue. It ought to be, it must be, I'll swear it's there.
Darnay (*suddenly*) Miss Manette, then!
Carton Miss Manette, then!

He drinks deep, staring at Darnay all the time, then flings his glass against the wall, where it shatters

That's a fair young lady to be pitied by and wept for by! How does it feel? Is it worth being tried for one's life, to be the object of such sympathy and compassion, Mr Darnay?
Darnay I — I cannot answer your question. I know that I am much indebted to you for your part in the happy outcome ...

Carton I neither want any thanks, nor merit any. It was nothing to do, in the first place; and I don't know why I did it in the second. Mr Darnay, let me ask you a question.
Darnay Willingly, and a small return for your good offices.
Carton Do you think I particularly like you?
Darnay Really Mr Carton, I have not asked myself the question.
Carton But ask yourself the question now.
Darnay (*after a pause*) You have acted as if you do, but I don't think you do ...
Carton I don't think I do. I begin to have a very good opinion of your understanding.
Darnay Nevertheless, there is nothing in that, I hope, to prevent our parting without ill-blood on either side ...
Carton Nothing in life!
Darnay Then *good-night*, Mr Carton. (*He makes to go*)
Carton (*stopping Darnay*) A last word, Mr Darnay; you think I am drunk?
Darnay I think you have been drinking.
Carton Think? You know I have been drinking.
Darnay Since I must say so, I know it.
Carton Then you shall likewise know why. I am a disappointed drudge, sir. I care for no man on earth, and no man on earth cares for me.
Darnay That is much to be regretted. (*A beat*) You might have used your talents better.
Carton May be so, Mr Darnay; may be not ...
Darnay Good-night then, Mr Carton.
Carton Good-night, good-night.

Darnay heads for the exit

Don't let your sober face elate you, however; you don't know what it may come to.

Darnay exits

Carton takes up a candle and examines himself by the light of it in a mirror. We become aware of other figures in the half-light watching him. Distant music; sad, serious

Do you particularly like the man? Why should you particularly like a man who resembles you? There is nothing in you to like; you know that. Ah confound you. What a change you have made in yourself! A good reason for taking to a man, that he shows you what you have fallen away from, and what you might have been! Change places with him, and would you have

Act I, Scene 9   27

been looked at by those blue eyes as he was, and commiserated by that agitated face as he was? Ah, the devil! Come on, and have it out in plain words — you hate the fellow!
First Onlooker And Sydney Carton turned, tossed his hat on, and walked out ...
Second Onlooker He turned into the Temple, and, having revived himself by twice pacing the pavements of King's Bench Walk and Paper Buildings, turned into the Stryver chambers ...

SCENE 9

The Jackal

A desk, books, a little pile of papers, an armchair, bottles. Firelight. Stryver in a great dressing-gown

Stryver You are a little late, Memory.
Carton About the usual time; it may be a quarter of an hour later. (*He removes his hat and coat*)

Bells sound the half-hour

Stryver Not much boiling down to be done tonight, Memory.
Carton How much?
Stryver Only two sets of them.
Carton Give me the worst first.
Stryver There they are, Sydney. Fire away.

And Carton takes them and throws them on to the table. During the Onlookers' commentary, he fetches a basin of water and towels, steeps the towels in the water, wrings them out and wraps them around his head. Stryver settles in the armchair. Carton buries himself in his papers. Both drink

First Onlooker It had been noted at the bar, that while Mr Stryver was a glib man, and an unscrupulous, and a ready, and a bold ——
Second Onlooker — he had not that faculty of extracting the essence from a heap of statements which is among the most striking and necessary of the advocate's accomplishments.
Third Onlooker But a remarkable improvement came upon him as to this.
First Onlooker So that at last it began to get about that although Sydney Carton would never be a lion, he was an amazingly good jackal, and that he rendered suit and service to Stryver in that capacity.
Second Onlooker Sometimes from ten at night until three in the damp dark morning.

And we hear a bell toll three. Slowly and damply. A pause. Papers are thrown down. A sigh

Stryver You were very sound, Sydney, in the matter of those witnesses today. Every question told.
Carton I always am sound; am I not?
Stryver I don't gainsay it. What has roughened your temper? Take some wine and smooth it again.

Carton does so

The old Sydney Carton of old Shrewsbury School — the old seesaw Sydney. Up one minute and down the next; now in spirits and now in despondency! Why?
Carton God knows. It is my way, I suppose.
Stryver Carton, your way is and always was a lame way. You summon no energy and no purpose. Look at me. How have I done what I have done? How do I do what I do?
Carton Partly through paying me to help you, I suppose. But what you want to do, you do. You were always in the front rank, and I was always behind.
Stryver I had to get into the front rank; I was not born there, was I?
Carton I was not present at the ceremony, but my opinion is — you were ... (*A beat*) But it's a gloomy thing to talk about one's past with the day breaking. Turn me in some other direction before I go.
Stryver Well then! Pledge me the pretty witness ... Are you turned in a pleasant direction now?
Carton (*grimly*) Pretty witness — I have had enough of pretty witnesses today. Who's your pretty witness?
Stryver The Doctor's daughter — Miss Manette.
Carton She pretty?
Stryver Is she not?
Carton No.
Stryver Why man alive, she was the admiration of the whole court!
Carton Rot the admiration of the whole court! Who made the Old Bailey a judge of beauty? She was a golden-haired doll!
Stryver Do you know, Sydney ... I rather thought, at the time, that you sympathized with the golden-haired doll ...
Carton Sympathized!? Great heavens above, man — I had more sympathy for your ugly face. Sympathy for her? Doll or no doll, I hardly noticed she was there. Absurd. I pledge you, but I deny the beauty. And now — now I'll have no more to drink: I'll go to bed. Good-night.

And Carton hurries out

Act I, Scene 10

The room vanishes. The street. Sad music

Mr Lorry When he got out of the house, the air was cold and sad, the dull sky overcast — and the river dark and dim. Waste forces within him and a desert all around, this man stood still for a moment, and saw, lying in the wilderness before him, a mirage of honourable ambition, self-denial, and perseverance.

Carton stops. A light shines into his face

Carton In the fair city of this vision, there were airy galleries from which the loves and graces looked upon him, gardens in which the fruits of life hung ripening, waters of hope that sparkled in his sight.
Mr Lorry A moment — and it was gone.

Carton climbs up and up through the network of passages and stairs. Music builds through this.

Climbing into a high chamber in a well of houses, he threw himself down in his clothes on a neglected bed, and its pillow was wet with wasted tears.

The Lights fade on Carton

SCENE 10

Gaspard's Child

Saint Antoine. A street sign for the wine shop appears

Down in the street, a group of figures begin to dance. One plays the violin, or an old pipe. It is a French tune, one that Mme Defarge hums from time to time, and the odd sample of broken-down humanity gathered in the street attempts a few moments of pleasure. There are children involved, represented by large rag dolls. They are passed from hand to hand. One is a little girl in ragged white. The dance is quaint — not the fierce choreography of the Terror. Defarge and Mme Defarge watch

In the distance, from the audience, the noise of a great coach and pounding hooves getting gradually closer. This noise competes with the music until the dancers can no longer ignore it. The dancers stare out in horror — frozen in the path of the approaching vehicle. Then they scatter, clutch at one another, turn this way and that. The Lights judder. A Light sweeps down across the audience. A screeching of brakes and whinnying of horses. Screams and shouts. We see the back of the coach halted just upstage. We see shadows of horses rearing and plunging. At the front of the stage the white doll lies, red and bloody. Gaspard, a tall man in a night-cap, rushes to the doll and picks it up. He howls over it like a wild animal

Gaspard Dead! DEAD!! She is dead! Killed, killed, killed!!

Defarge comes forward to comfort Gaspard. As he does so, a figure emerges from the coach and stands looking down at the crowd. It is the Marquis St Evrémonde: about sixty now, with a face like a fine mask. Handsome, cruel

Marquis What has gone wrong?
Defarge It is his child.
Marquis It is extraordinary to me that you people cannot take care of yourselves and your children. One or the other of you is forever in the way. How do I know what injury you have done to my horses? Here: give him that.

And he flings down a coin for Defarge to give to Gaspard. It rolls and tinkles on the ground. Everyone stares in silence

Gaspard (*a terrible cry*) DEAD!!
Defarge Be a brave man, Gaspard. It is better for the poor little plaything to die so, than to live. It has died in a moment without pain. Could it have lived an hour as happily?
Marquis (*smiling*) You are a philosopher. How do they call you?
Defarge They call me Defarge.
Marquis Of what trade?
Defarge Monsieur the Marquis — vendor of wine.
Marquis Pick up that, philosopher and vendor of wine, and spend it as you will. (*He throws another gold coin*) The horses there! Are they settled? (*And he turns to climb back into the coach*)

A low murmur from the crowd. We can make out the word "revenge". The Marquis's ease is suddenly disturbed by a coin flying into his carriage

Who threw that? (*Silence*) You dogs. I would ride over any of you very willingly and exterminate you from the earth. If I knew which of you threw at the carriage, and had a mind to teach you a lesson you should be crushed under the wheels. (*He climbs into the carriage and calls out*) GO ON!

And the carriage moves away

Silence — except for sobbing Gaspard, and the click, click of Mme Defarge's needles

Defarge (*tense*) It is a long time.

Act I, Scene 10

Mme Defarge And when is it not a long time? Vengeance and retribution require a long time; it is the rule.
Defarge It does not take a long time to strike a man with lightning.

Murmurs of agreement from the crowd

Mme Defarge (*stopping her knitting and turning to face the crowd*) How long does it take to make and store lightning? Tell me! (*Silence*) It does not take a long time for an earthquake to swallow a town. Tell me how long it takes to prepare an earthquake.
Defarge A long time.
Mme Defarge But when it is ready, it takes place, and grinds to pieces everything before it. In the meantime, it is always preparing, though it is not seen or heard. That is your consolation. Keep it. (*She moves among the crowd*) Look around and consider the lives of all the world that we know, consider the faces of all the world that we know, consider the rage and discontent which you feel more and more in your hearts every hour. Can such things last?!
Gaspard (*faintly*) But it may not come during our lives.
Mme Defarge We shall have helped it. Nothing that we do is done in vain. I believe with all my soul that we shall see the triumph. But even if not — there is not a debt outstanding that I would not pay with interest. (*She stares steadily and unblinkingly at Gaspard*)
Gaspard (*looking back into Mme Defarge's eyes*) Yes. Of course. Yes.

And he turns and goes, cradling the dead child

Mme Defarge (*to the rest of the crowd*) When the time comes, let loose a tiger and a devil; but wait for the time with the tiger and the devil chained, not shown, yet always ready.

Murmurs of assent, agreement

(*Holding up the stuff she is knitting*) Return to your homes. The day is coming when this pattern shall be plainly understood, and every name recorded here unpicked.

The crowd disperse. During the following, the Lights come down to focus on the pair and the crowd's footsteps echo beneath the dialogue

Defarge (*approaching Mme Defarge*) My brave wife. (*Beat*) I have been warned: there is another spy commissioned for our quarter.
Mme Defarge Eh well! It is necessary to register him. How do they call this man?

Defarge He is English.
Mme Defarge So much the better. His name?
Defarge Barsad.
Mme Defarge Barsad. Good. Christian name?
Defarge John.
Mme Defarge John Barsad. Good. His appearance, is it known?
Defarge Age about forty, average height, black hair, rather handsome visage, dark complexion, brown eyes, face long and sallow.
Mme Defarge Eh my faith, it is a portrait. (*Laughing*) He shall be registered tomorrow.

The footsteps grow louder, and echo and fade and grow again, and cross and recross

The pair listen, and the Lights go out on them

Scene 11

Soho

During the following, the Lights come up on a network of bright summer rooms. A large plane tree outside. Dappled shade. Birdsong. Still the sound of footsteps in and around the streets. The atmosphere is no longer threatening. Upstage, half turned away from us, sits Dr Manette, at a table laid for dinner. Darnay sits near him. Carton is slumped by a window out of which he stares moodily

Mr Lorry The quiet lodgings of Dr Manette — and his daughter Lucie — were in a quiet street corner not far from Soho Square.
Dr Manette There were few buildings then, north of the Oxford Road, and forest trees flourished and wild flowers grew, and the hawthorn blossomed in the now vanished fields.
Lucie As a consequence, country airs circulated in Soho with vigorous freedom, instead of languishing into the parish like stray paupers without a settlement.

Miss Pross enters

Miss Pross Miss Pross ——
Mr Lorry — a pleasant sight, albeit wild and red and grim ——
Miss Pross (*grimly*) Miss *Pross* ——
Mr Lorry Who had escorted her young charge Lucie to meet Mr Lorry at Dover nearly six years earlier.

Act I, Scene 11   33

Miss Pross Miss Pross took charge of the little household ——
Mr Lorry — and always acquitted herself marvellously ...
Miss Pross (*glowing*) Her dinners — of a modest quality — were well-cooked and well-served. She ravaged Soho in search of impoverished French, who, for a shilling, would impart culinary mysteries to her.
Mr Lorry Mr Lorry was a frequent visitor ...
Miss Pross (*sharply*) How do you do.
Mr Lorry I am pretty well, I thank you. How are you?
Miss Pross Nothing to boast of ——
Mr Lorry Indeed?
Miss Pross Ah! Indeed!
Mr Lorry Miss Pross, I have a question for you ——
Miss Pross (*ignoring him*) I am very much put out about my Ladybird.
Mr Lorry Indeed?
Miss Pross For gracious sake say something else besides "indeed" or you'll fidget me to death.
Mr Lorry (*amused*) Really, then?
Miss Pross Really is bad enough, but better. Yes — I am very much put out.
Mr Lorry May I ask the cause?
Miss Pross I don't want dozens of people who are not at all worthy of Ladybird, to come here looking after her!
Mr Lorry Do dozens come for that purpose?
Miss Pross Hundreds!
Mr Lorry Dear me!

Lucie appears from the kitchen with a jug of water and a bottle of wine for Dr Manette and Darnay. Carton has been waiting for her

Carton (*to Lucie*) If I could speak with you alone.
Darnay (*at a distance, unaware of Carton*) Lucie!
Carton (*urgently*) For just two minutes ...
Darnay (*as before*) Lucie!

With a look of helpless apology to Carton, Lucie turns and goes to Darnay. Miserably, Carton sinks back into his chair

Miss Pross (*more than ever disturbed by these rival bids for Lucie's attention*) I have lived with the darling — and she has paid me for it which she certainly should never have done — since she was ten years old. And it's really very hard. *Crowds* and *multitudes* of people who are not in the least worthy of the pet are always turning up to take Ladybird's affections away from me! When you began it ——
Mr Lorry (*astonished*) *I* began it Miss Pross?

Miss Pross Didn't you? *Who brought her father to life!?* Not that I have any fault to find with Dr Manette, except that he is not worthy of such a daughter.
Mr Lorry It is of the Doctor that I wish to speak.
Miss Pross (*crossly*) Hey ho hum! (*And she bustles off to join Dr Manette, Darnay and Lucie at the dinner table*)

After a moment, Mr Lorry follows her. Carton, left alone in the foreground, paces restlessly. During this, a burst of laughter from the table

Lucie ... you must not say such things — even in jest!
Dr Manette Indeed, Charles Darnay, you shall not leave us tomorrow. I forbid it!
Darnay I shall be in France for only a month.
Lucie Then it will be in a month's time that I shall next pass a night untroubled by anxieties for your safety.
Darnay You see? I am a villain. The prosecution case was fair ...

More laughter and conversation at the table. Lucie breaks away, and, concerned for Carton, moves to him

Lucie (*after a few moments' embarrassed silence*) Mr Carton? You said you wished to speak to me?
Carton I did.
Lucie You have eaten nothing, Mr Carton. I fear you are not well.
Carton No. But the life I lead, Miss Manette, is not conducive to health. What is to be expected of — or by — such profligates?
Lucie (*surprised*) Perhaps ... Perhaps you should try to live a better life.
Carton God knows it is a shame.
Lucie Then why not change it?

He turns away, fighting tears. Mr Lorry, mindful that Lucie may need to be "rescued", appears from upstage

Mr Lorry Lucie, we are losing ground with Mr Darnay. You alone can dissuade him.
Lucie I think not. You must fight on without me. At least for a few minutes ...

Mr Lorry understands that she wishes to be left alone with Carton. He withdraws

Carton I break down before the knowledge of what I want to say to you. Will you hear me?

Act I, Scene 11   35

Lucie If it will do you any good, Mr Carton, it would make me very glad.
Carton Thank you.

A moment passes

    Don't be afraid to hear me. Don't shrink from anything I say.

Another beat

    I am like one who died young. All my life might have been.
Lucie No, Mr Carton, I am sure that the best part of it might still be. You deserve so much more.
Carton Say, I deserve you, Miss Manette, say I am worthy of you, and although I know better, although in the mystery of my own wretched heart I know better, I shall never forget it.
Lucie (*deeply surprised*) Mr Carton — I ...

A long, difficult moment

Carton (*turning away*) I know very well that you can have no tenderness for me. I ask for none. I am even thankful that it cannot be ... If it had been possible for you to return the love of the man you see before you, he would have been conscious in spite of his happiness that he would blight you, disgrace you, pull you down with him.
Lucie (*the agony of knowing pity is all she can offer*) Can I not repay this confidence by turning it to some good account for yourself?
Carton To none. No, Miss Manette, to none.
Lucie Can I not save you, Mr Carton?
Carton I wish you to know that you have been the last dream of my soul. The sight of you with your father, and of this home made such a home by you, has stirred old shadows that I thought had died out of me. Since I knew you, I have been troubled by a remorse that I thought would never trouble me again. I have had ideas of striving afresh, beginning anew, shaking off sloth and sensuality and fighting out the abandoned fight. A dream, all a dream that ends in nothing and leaves the sleeper where he lay down, but I wish you to know that you inspired it.
Lucie Have I no power for good with you at all?
Carton The utmost good of which I am capable now, Miss Manette, I have come here to realize. Let me carry through the rest of my misdirected life the remembrance that I opened my heart to you — and that there was something left in me which you could deplore and pity.
Lucie Which I entreat you to believe, with all my heart, was capable of better things.

Carton (*urgent, bitter*) Entreat me to believe it no more, Miss Manette. I have proved myself, and I know better. (*A beat*) I have spoken to you in confidence.
Lucie (*heartfelt*) Mr Carton — the secret is yours not mine; and I promise to respect it.
Carton Thank you and God bless you. Be under no misapprehension Miss Manette, of my ever resuming this conversation by so much as a passing word. Within myself I shall always be, towards you, what I am now, but outwardly I shall be what you have hitherto seen.
Lucie I believe you. I believe you.
Carton (*brokenly*) For you, and for any dear to you, I would do anything, I would embrace any sacrifice ...

But they are interrupted. Miss Pross hurries up

Miss Pross (*pointedly*) The custard will be growing mould if we do not end all this conversing in corners and sit down at the table to eat it! This is an improper retirement.
Carton (*edging away; muttering*) I will relieve you of a visitor — a visitor between whom and you there is an impassable space ...
Lucie Mr Carton!

He exits to the front door; she follows him

Mr Lorry (*seeing that at last his moment has come*) Miss Pross ...
Miss Pross (*upset*) It is *doubly* and *trebly* hard for a person, when they have performed their appointed task and made eggs do their business in a foreign pastry, to find other persons scurrying up and down like ants on a doorstep!
Mr Lorry (*determined*) My dear Miss Pross ...
Miss Pross (*fretful*) Your dear Miss Nobody!
Mr Lorry I have a question for you.
Miss Pross And I shall have *a fit of the jerks* shall keep me in my room for a week!
Mr Lorry We are both people of business ...
Miss Pross People of stuff and nonsense!
Mr Lorry Let me ask you — for you alone I can trust in this — does the doctor never refer to the shoemaking time?
Miss Pross (*interested in spite of herself*) Never.
Mr Lorry And yet he keeps the bench and the tools beside him?
Miss Pross Well?
Mr Lorry Do you believe he thinks of it much?
Miss Pross I do.
Mr Lorry Do you imagine —— ?

Act I, Scene 11

Miss Pross Never imagine anything. Have no imagination at all!
Mr Lorry I stand corrected; do you suppose — you go so far as to suppose sometimes?
Miss Pross Now and then.
Mr Lorry Good! Do you suppose Dr Manette has any theory of his own, preserved through all these years, about the cause of his being oppressed; perhaps even to the name of his oppressor?
Miss Pross I don't suppose anything about it but what Ladybird tells me.
Mr Lorry And that is?
Miss Pross That she thinks he has!
Mr Lorry It is remarkable that Dr Manette should never touch upon the question.
Miss Pross Well. To the best of my understanding — and bad's the best you'll tell me — he is afraid of the whole subject.
Mr Lorry Afraid?
Miss Pross It's plain enough. His loss of himself grew out of it. Not knowing how he lost himself, or how he recovered himself, he may never feel certain of not losing himself again.
Mr Lorry (*impressed by her perspicacity*) True. And fearful to reflect upon.
Miss Pross Sometimes he gets up in the dead of night and will be heard walking up and down, walking up and down in his room. Ladybird has learnt to know then that his mind is walking up and down, walking up and down in his old prison.

Darnay and Dr Manette are seen getting up from the table

Mr Lorry (*sotto voce*) Here he is. We shall continue our discussion in the kitchen. (*Improvizing for Dr Manette's benefit*) Show me your custard, Pross!

And they go

Dr Manette arrives, followed by Darnay. The middle of a difficult conversation. A few moments pass

Darnay Shall I go on, sir?
Dr Manette (*after a blank silence*) Yes, go on.
Darnay Dear Dr Manette, you must believe it. I love your daughter dearly, disinterestedly, devotedly. If ever there were love in the world, I love her. You have loved yourself; let your old love speak for me ——
Manette (*deeply anguished*) NO!

A moment passes

I ask your pardon. I do not doubt your loving Lucie, you may be satisfied of that. Have you spoken to her of marriage?

Darnay (*after a moment*) There is a tenderness between you and Miss Manette so unusual and so touching, that I have felt, and do even now feel, that to bring my love between you is to touch your history with something not quite so good as itself. But I love her. Heaven is my witness that I love her.

Dr Manette I believe it.

Darnay I look only to sharing your life and home, not to come between you and Lucie but to bind her closer to you if such a thing can be.

Dr Manette You speak feelingly and honestly. I thank you for that. (*Then, hesitantly, "with obvious distress"*) If there were any ... apprehensions against the man she really loved, they should all be obliterated for her sake. She is everything to me; more to me than suffering, more to me than wrong, more to me ... Well. This is idle talk. (*A deep breath*) Charles Darnay, I will not stand in your way.

Darnay (*deeply moved*) Dr Manette, I thank you. (*A moment*) Your confidence in me ought to be returned with full confidence on my part. (*Another moment*) My present name, though but slightly changed, is not my own. I wish to tell you what it is, and why I am in England ...

Dr Manette (*sharply*) Stop!

Darnay I wish it, that I may the better deserve your confidence ——

Music begins

Dr Manette (*with real fear*) Stop! (*A long moment*) Tell me when I ask you, not now. If your suit should prosper, if Lucie should love you, you shall tell me on your wedding day.

And the music which underscores this last speech rises up

Manette leaves Darnay and climbs up to his room

Lucie returns and goes to Darnay

The Lights fade, and we hear ... carriage wheels again, pounding hooves and the crack of the driver's whip

SCENE 12

The Nephew of the Marquis

We catch glimpses of a long journey

Coachman Monsieur the Marquis was driven on from the Suburb of St Antoine.

Act I, Scene 12   39

Postilion A blush on the countenance of Monsieur the Marquis was no impeachment of his high breeding ...
Coachman It was occasioned by an external circumstance beyond his control ——
Postilion — the setting sun.

We see the Marquis in his carriage, momentarily steeped in crimson

Marquis It will die out — directly.

And it does

Coachman At last the carriage arrived at a poor village near the Château of Monsieur the Marquis. And stopped.
Marquis You there! Come here!

A Peasant scurries to the coach door

I passed you on the road?
Peasant Monseigneur, it is true. I had the honour of being passed on the road.
Marquis What did you look at so fixedly?
Peasant Monseigneur, I looked at the man.
Marquis What man, Pig?
Peasant Pardon, Monseigneur, he hung under the carriage.
Marquis Who?
Peasant Monseigneur, the man!
Marquis The devil take these idiots! Who was he?
Peasant Of all the days of my life, I never saw him.
Marquis What was he like?
Peasant Monseigneur, he was whiter than the miller. All covered with dust. White as a spectre ... tall as a spectre!

A beat. Perhaps we momentarily glimpse the pale figure of Gaspard

Marquis (*shouting to the Coachman*) Go on!

And the carriage moves off

Coachman The carriage broke into a brisk trot, and Monseigneur ——
Postilion — escorted by the furies ——
Coachman — rapidly diminished the league or two of distance that remained between him and his dinner.

Postilion At last the carriage stopped.
Coachman Up the broad flight of shallow steps, Monsieur the Marquis, flambeau preceded, went to the great door of his château.

We see the Marquis and a servant — Gabelle — move through the house

Marquis Has my nephew arrived?
Gabelle No, Monseigneur.
Marquis He will arrive tonight. Leave the table where it is.

They have arrived at a heavily laden table. Gabelle removes the Marquis's coat and gloves

Gabelle In a quarter of an hour, Monseigneur was ready ——
Marquis — and sat down to a light supper.
Gabelle Suddenly ——

A noise. A hand scrabbling, a fall of pebbles. A shadow passes over the stage

Marquis (*calmly*) What was that?
Gabelle Monseigneur?
Marquis Outside the window.

Gabelle goes to the window, opens it, looks outside

Well?
Gabelle Monseigneur, it is nothing. The trees and night are all that are here.
Marquis Good.

But suddenly the noise of a carriage

Gabelle He was half-way through his supper when he heard the sound of wheels.

Another servant appears

Servant It is your nephew, Monseigneur.
Gabelle (*to the audience*) He had been a few leagues behind Monseigneur ...
Servant — had diminished the distance rapidly ——
Gabelle — had heard of Monseigneur at the posting-houses as being before him ——
Servant — was to be told that supper awaited him ——

Act I, Scene 12

Gabelle — was prayed to come to it.
Servant (*at the door*) He had been known in England as —— (*He opens the door*) Mr Charles Darnay!

Darnay enters, bows to his uncle, then suddenly sees Gabelle

Darnay (*delighted*) Gabelle, my dear old friend.
Gabelle Good Master Charles!
Darnay I had hardly dared to hope that I should see you!
Marquis (*frostily*) Thank you, Gabelle. Stay outside. I shall ring for you.

Gabelle leaves

Ever the friend of servants, Monsieur Charles.
Darnay I have answered your summons. I have come back, sir, as you requested ——
Marquis Eventually.
Darnay — but still pursuing the object that took me away. It carried me into great and unexpected peril; but it is a sacred object, and if it had carried me to death I hope it would have sustained me.
Marquis (*smiling*) Not to death ... it is not necessary to say "to death" ...
Darnay I doubt, sir, whether if it had carried me to the utmost brink of death you would have cared to stop me there.
Marquis (*pleasantly*) No no no ...
Darnay Indeed I believe it to be at once your bad fortune and my good fortune that has kept me out of a prison in France.
Marquis Dare I ask you to explain.
Darnay I believe that if you were not in disgrace with the Court, and had not been overshadowed by that cloud for years past, a *lettre de cachet* would have sent me to some fortress indefinitely.
Marquis (*calmly*) It is possible. (*A beat*) But I am — as you say — at a disadvantage. These little instruments of correction, these gentle aids to the power and honour of families, are only to be obtained now by interest and importunity. We have lost many privileges, and the assertion of our station in these days might cause us real inconvenience. All very bad, very bad! (*An exquisite pinch of snuff*)
Darnay (*controlling his anger*) We have so asserted our station that I believe our name to be more detested than any name in France.
Marquis Let us hope so. Detestation of the high is the involuntary homage of the low.
Darnay There is not a face I can look at in all the country round about us, which looks at me with any deference on it but the dark deference of fear and slavery.

Marquis A compliment to the grandeur of the family, merited by the manner in which the family has sustained its grandeur.
Darnay A manner requiring that we injure every human creature who came between us and our pleasure. And I am left to execute the last request of my dear mother's lips and to obey the last look of her eyes, which implored me to have mercy and to redress.
Marquis (*smiling*) Better to be a rational creature and accept your natural destiny. But you are lost, Monsieur Charles, I see.
Darnay The inheritance and title are lost to me — I renounce them. If they passed to me from you, I would abandon them and live otherwise and elsewhere. What is this property but a crumbling tower of waste, mismanagement, oppression, hunger and suffering.
Marquis And you? Forgive my curiosity; how do you, under your new philosophy, graciously intend to live?
Darnay I shall work.
Marquis In England, for example.
Darnay Yes.
Marquis They say, these boastful English, that it is the refuge of many. (*Beat*) You know a compatriot who has found refuge there? A doctor?
Darnay (*taken aback*) Yes ...
Marquis With a daughter?
Darnay Yes?
Marquis Yes. A doctor with a daughter. Yes. So commences the new philosophy. You are fatigued. Good-night!
Darnay Uncle! What interest might they be of yours?!
Marquis Good-night. I look forward to the pleasure of seeing you again in the morning. Good repose. (*Calling*) Gabelle! Light Monsieur my nephew to his chamber there ——

And Gabelle shows Darnay out

— and burn Monsieur my nephew in his bed, if you will ...

The Marquis climbs a flight of stairs to his bedroom. We hear a tune — elegant and sinister — picked out on a harpsichord perhaps

First Narrator Monsieur the Marquis walked to and fro in his loose chamber robe to prepare himself for sleep that hot, still night.
Second Narrator Rustling about the room, his soft slippered feet making no noise on the floor, he moved like a refined tiger.

The Narrators withdraw. The Lights dim slightly. From about the darkened room we hear whispers — "Revenge, revenge"

Act I, Scene 13   43

The Marquis continues his prowling dance. The music plays on. He goes to the great window and pulls back the curtain. He stares out into the night. Suddenly some particularly dark piece of night seems to gather around him, and he stiffens, appears suddenly still. Slowly he turns back to us. His elegant throat has been cut. Blood cascades down his white shirt. He cannot speak or scream. His face contorts violently. A strange, rough voice cries out

Voice *Drive him fast to his tomb!*

The Marquis reaches out, clutches the curtain, falls. Immediately, with his body still well in view —

Scene 13

Wedding Bells

Bells ring out. We see Lorry and Miss Pross with Lucie in a "quiet, pretty" bridal dress. In the foreground Darnay stands alone with Dr Manette. The body of the Marquis drips a little blood from above. We can still make out the weird harpsichord music of the prowling dance

Darnay It is time.
Dr Manette Yes.
Darnay I must fulfil my promise to you and tell you the whole truth of my history.
Dr Manette Yes.
Darnay So nothing stands between us.

And they turn away

First Narrator And on the morning of his marriage day ——
Second Narrator — Charles Darnay told the good doctor of Beauvais ——
First Narrator — where he had been born and why he was in England ——
Second Narrator — the nature of his lifelong quest and of the obligations that bound him to it.
First Narrator But most importantly he told the doctor his name ——
Second Narrator — and who his father had been.

The harpsichord music fades. The bloody figure of the Marquis rises to his feet, and smiling grimly — addresses the audience

Marquis And who his uncle was —— His Grace, the late and greatly unlamented Marquis St Evrémonde!

And the dead Marquis bows low, turns and leaves

Lucie comes down, and holds hands with Darnay. They face Dr Manette

Dr Manette (*apparently calm*) Take her, Charles, she is yours.

The lovers embrace. Miss Pross and Lorry shower them with confetti. Lucie and Darnay leave, Dr Manette starts to climb the stairs to his room. Lorry turns to Miss Pross

Mr Lorry Don't cry.
Miss Pross I am not crying, you are.
Mr Lorry I, my Pross?
Miss Pross You were just now; I saw you do it.
Mr Lorry Dear me, dear me. Perhaps I was. This is an occasion that makes a man speculate on all he has lost. To think there might have been a Mrs Lorry any time these fifty years almost!
Miss Pross Not at all!!
Mr Lorry You think there never might have been a Mrs Lorry?
Miss Pross Pooh! You were a bachelor in your cradle.
Mr Lorry (*beaming*) Well!! That seems probable too.
Miss Pross And you were cut out for a bachelor before you were put in your cradle!
Mr Lorry Then I think that I was very unhandsomely dealt with, and that I ought to have had a voice in the selection of my pattern!

Suddenly, from the shadows above, we hear the tap tap tap of a hammer. We can just see Dr Manette, back turned to us, now in his old threadbare jacket, crouched over the workbench; Lorry turns to Miss Pross in horror

Mr Lorry Good God! What's that?
Miss Pross (*appalled*) Ah me! We are lost!
Mr Lorry Follow me ... quickly!

And they turn to climb the stairs

Scene 14

What follows is a split scene. As Lorry and Miss Pross move up, Mme Defarge moves into sight down below. The lower level is now the wineshop in St Antoine. The hammering above counterpoints a knocking on the counter. It is Barsad

Barsad Good-day, Madame.

Act I, Scene 14   45

Mme Defarge Good-day, Monsieur.
Barsad Have the goodness to give me a little glass of old Cognac and a mouthful of cool fresh water, Madame.
Mme Defarge (*moving to pour the drinks; to herself*) Good-day age about forty, good-day average height, good-day black hair, handsome visage, dark complexion, brown eyes, sallow face ... Good-day, one and all ... (*And she brings the glass to him*)
Barsad (*drinking*) How is business?
Mme Defarge Very bad. The people are so poor.
Barsad Ah, the unfortunate, miserable people, so oppressed too — as you say.
Mme Defarge As *you* say ...
Barsad Of course. But you naturally think so. Of course.
Mme Defarge I *think*? I have enough to do to keep this wine shop open without thinking. All we think here is how to live. I think for others? No, no. You must speak to my husband. He will return shortly ...

And Barsad drinks on

Above, Lorry is with the Doctor. Miss Pross holds back

Mr Lorry Dr Manette. My dear friend, Dr Manette!
Dr Manette (*muttering*) Work to be done.
Mr Lorry Dr Manette — think where you are, think what you do!
Dr Manette A young lady's walking shoe ... where is it ... it ought to have been finished long ago ... I must find it ...
Mr Lorry You know me, my dear friend?
Dr Manette What did you say?
Mr Lorry I beg you, think again. This is not your proper occupation. Think, dear friend!

But Dr Manette simply hammers away at his bench

Downstairs, Defarge arrives

Barsad Good-day Monsieur.
Defarge Good-day ...

Beat

Barsad Bad business, this, of Gaspard's execution.
Defarge Gaspard?
Barsad The father of the dead child.
Defarge Many children die in these streets, Monsieur.

Barsad The child cruelly slain by Monsieur the Marquis, himself cruelly slain by the dead child's father.
Defarge So they say.
Barsad They built a gallows by the village fountain. Forty feet high. On the top of the gallows they fixed a knife, blade upwards, with its point in the air. He hangs there still, poisoning the water.
Mme Defarge He knew beforehand what the price of his luxury was; he has paid the price.
Barsad I believe there is much compassion and anger in the neighbourhood touching the poor fellow. Between ourselves.
Defarge Is there?
Barsad Is there not?
Defarge (*sweetly*) We have not heard of it.

Stalemate. The focus shifts back to Soho. Dr Manette taps away at his bench. Miss Pross and Lorry confer anxiously

Miss Pross If only my Ladybird were here ...
Mr Lorry No! This must be kept a secret from Lucie at all costs.
Miss Pross A secret?
Mr Lorry It is her honeymoon. (*Beat*) Write to her!
Miss Pross A letter?
Mr Lorry Describing his having been called away.
Miss Pross In his present condition?
Mr Lorry No no no ... *pretend* he has been called away.
Miss Pross (*horrified*) Deceive my Ladybird!?
Mr Lorry A *kind* deception.
Miss Pross But called away by whom?
Mr Lorry Called away professionally.
Miss Pross (*conspiratorial*) Ahh!
Mr Lorry I shall, for the first time in my life, absent myself from Tellson's. I must stay always with him, reading and writing and so forth. He must see this is a free place.

Miss Pross hurries off to write her letter

Lorry settles himself and opens a book. Dr Manette stitches

And in St Antoine, Defarge arrives at the counter. Barsad looks up

Barsad The pleasure of conversing with you, Monsieur Defarge, recalls to me that I have the honour of cherishing some interesting associations with your name.

Act I, Scene 14   47

Defarge Indeed?
Barsad Yes indeed. When Dr Manette was released, you had the charge of him, I know. He was delivered to you. You see, I am informed of the circumstances ...
Defarge Such is the fact, certainly.
Barsad It was to you that his daughter came, and it was from your care that she took him over to England.
Defarge Such is the fact.
Barsad She is lately married.
Mme Defarge Only lately? She was pretty enough to have been married long ago. You English are cold, it seems to me.
Barsad (*disconcerted*) Oh, you know I am English ...
Mme Defarge I perceive your tongue is ...

A beat

Barsad Yes, Miss Manette is to be married — to one who like herself is French by birth. It is a curious thing: her husband is the nephew of Monsieur the Marquis, for whom poor Gaspard was exalted to so great a height — in other words, the present Marquis. He lives unknown in England. Mr Charles Darnay he calls himself.
Defarge (*despite himself*) No, no!
Mme Defarge (*completely calm*) We are grateful for this news of an old acquaintance, and naturally happy for her happiness. (*Sweetly*) Another cognac for Monsieur?
Barsad No. No thank you, I must take my leave. But I look forward to the pleasure of seeing Monsieur and Madame Defarge again.

Mme Defarge smiles, inclines her head

Barsad pays and goes

Defarge (*nervous*) Can it be true? What he said of Ma'm'selle Manette?
Mme Defarge As he has said it, it is probably false, but it may be true.
Defarge If it is?
Mme Defarge If it is?
Defarge And we live to see the great reckoning, I hope, for her sake, destiny will keep her husband out of France.
Mme Defarge Her husband's destiny will take him where he is to go, and will lead him to the end that is to end him.
Defarge But is it not very strange, that after all our sympathy for Dr Manette and his daughter, her husband's name should be proscribed under your hand at this moment, by the side of that accursed spy who has just left us ...?

Mme Defarge Stranger things than that will happen when it does come. I have them both here of a certainty, and they are both here for their merits, that is enough.

Madame Defarge rolls up her knitting and retires to the back of the shop. Defarge follows

SCENE 15

A Recovery

Upstairs, the Light finds Mr Lorry dozing, and no sign of Dr Manette. The shoemaker's bench and tools are tidied away

Narrator The third day came and went, the fourth, the fifth. Five days, six days, seven days, eight days, nine days. With a hope ever darkening, and with a heart always growing heavier and heavier, Mr Lorry passed through this anxious time. The shoemaker was growing dreadfully skilful, and his hands ever more nimble and expert ...

There is a knock at the door

Mr Lorry (*starting*) What?! Where? Yes ... of course ... come in!

Miss Pross enters

Miss Pross (*whispering*) Shall I bring his breakfast now?
Mr Lorry Yes indeed, my dear Pross, everything as normal ——

He is stopped in his tracks by a loud squawk from Miss Pross

Are you quite well?
Miss Pross (*pointing*) Gone!
Mr Lorry (*aghast*) Dr Manette!!
Miss Pross Dead!
Mr Lorry Miss Pross!
Miss Pross He threw himself from the window!
Mr Lorry What?
Miss Pross His poor body broken on the stones below! (*She is overcome*)
Mr Lorry (*at the window*) No sign of it ...
Miss Pross Somebody swept him up!
Mr Lorry Nonsense!

The door opens and Dr Manette enters. Well-dressed, calm, pale, collected

Act I, Scene 15   49

Dr Manette Good-morning, Mr Lorry. Pross.
Mr Lorry Er ... Dr Manette ...?
Dr Manette I have been downstairs. Is it not time for breakfast?
Mr Lorry Why yes — *yes* it is! Pross! What are you thinking of?
Miss Pross Well my blessed Aunt Betsy.
Dr Manette Have you stayed the night with us, Mr Lorry? Perhaps the excitement of the wedding fatigued you ...?
Miss Pross But the wedding ...
Mr Lorry *Exactly!* The wedding. (*Gesturing*) Breakfast, Pross — as usual in the dining-room.

She goes

Well. What a happy day this is. Happy that is for a Wednesday ...
Dr Manette (*uneasily*) But it is surely Sunday.
Mr Lorry Wednesday for sure. The first Wednesday of August. Now, shall we go down?
Dr Manette The first Wednesday of August?
Mr Lorry Why yes.
Dr Manette Impossible ...
Mr Lorry No, I assure you.
Dr Manette But only yesterday ...
Mr Lorry Ten days ago ...
Dr Manette How can this be?
Mr Lorry Oh my dear friend!
Dr Manette (*shocked*) A relapse ... There has been a relapse.
Mr Lorry Slight! Very slight ...
Dr Manette Of how long duration?
Mr Lorry Nine days and nights.
Dr Manette How did it show itself? (*Looking at his hands*) In the resumption of an old pursuit?
Mr Lorry That is the fact.
Dr Manette I dreaded this.
Mr Lorry Could a repetition be prevented? (*Beat*) If you had confided in us ...
Dr Manette Impossible. You can have no idea how difficult it is to say a word upon the subject ...
Mr Lorry But if we knew the cause of the attack ...
Dr Manette (*slowly*) I think that some intense associations of a most distressing nature were vividly recalled.
Mr Lorry But for the future ...
Dr Manette The future? Dear Mr Lorry, I hope and almost believe that the circumstances likely to renew the disorder are exhausted.

Mr Lorry So. (*Beat*) Forgive me, as a persistent man of business ... may I ask you one further question?

Dr Manette nods

Is it not a pity that you should have the instruments of your old occupation about you?

A beat. Dr Manette looks away. Taps his foot nervously

If the tools of your old trade were gone, my dear Manette, might not some of the old fear go with them?
Dr Manette You see ... it is very hard to explain. It was so welcome once ——
Mr Lorry I would not keep them.
Dr Manette — when there was nothing. Nothing!
Mr Lorry They do no good now ... come. For Lucie's sake.
Dr Manette For Lucie's sake then. Let it be done ...

Miss Pross bustles in

Miss Pross Five days later, in good health and tranquil state of mind, Dr Manette went away to join Lucie and her husband ...

Dr Manette goes

The Lights darken. Mr Lorry and Miss Pross climb the stairs

Miss Pross That same night, Mr Lorry went into the Doctor's room with an axe, saw, chisel and hammer, attended by Miss Pross carrying a light.
Mr Lorry There, with closed doors, and in a mysterious and guilty manner, Mr Lorry hacked the shoemaker's bench to pieces ——
Miss Pross While Miss Pross held the candle as if she were assisting at a murder ...
Mr Lorry For which indeed in her grimness she was no unsuitable figure!

Scene 16

A scene that takes us through seven years. The music that underscores begins sunny enough, though it always has a watchful ticking quality about it. Perhaps footsteps patter through it (as Dickens indicates in Chapter 20 of the second book). By the end of this scene, the music is sinister and threatening. A fine day has turned dark and stormy

Act I, Scene 16 51

Lucie When the newly married pair came home, the first person who appeared to offer his congratulations was Sydney Carton.
Carton (*to Darnay*) Mr Darnay, I wish we might be friends.
Darnay We are already friends, I hope.
Carton Ha! Fashion of speech.
Darnay No! Mr Carton!
Carton You remember a famous occasion when I was drunk? More drunk than usual ...
Darnay I remember a certain famous occasion when you forced me to confess that you had been drinking.
Carton The curse of such occasions lies heavy on me for I always remember them. I wish you would forget it.
Darnay I forgot it long ago.
Carton Fashion of speech again, Mr Darnay. But oblivion is not so easy for me and a light answer does not help me to forget it.
Darnay Have I nothing more important to remember than the great service you rendered me that day?
Carton Mere professional claptrap.
Darnay You make light of the obligation. But I will not quarrel with your light answer.
Carton I have gone aside from my purpose. I was speaking about our being friends.
Darnay Yes.
Carton You know me. Dissolute dog. Never done any good. Never will.
Darnay I don't know that you never will.
Carton I do. Take my word for it. Well! If you could endure to have such a worthless fellow coming and going at odd times, I should ask that I might be permitted ... (*wryly*) ... as a privileged person. I doubt I should abuse the permission. Might avail myself of it four times a year. It would satisfy me I dare say to know that I had it.
Darnay (*warmly*) Will you try?
Carton Thank you. I thank you, Darnay. (*He turns to go, then turns back*) I may use that freedom with your name?
Darnay I think so, Carton, by this time.

And Carton goes

Lucie approaches

Lucie You seem thoughtful.
Darnay He doesn't care. About himself, about the world. He keeps to no path, travels in no intended direction. He seems incapable of all the higher, better flights of men.

Lucie Be generous with him always. He has a heart he very, very seldom reveals, and there are deep wounds in it. But I am sure that he is capable of good things, gentle things, even magnanimous things.
Darnay I will always remember it.

Darnay and Lucie embrace

Mr Lorry A wonderful corner for echoes, that corner where the doctor lived. Ever busily winding the golden thread which bound her husband and her father and herself and her old companion in a life of quiet bliss, Lucie sat in the still house, in the tranquilly resounding corner, listening to the echoing footsteps of years.

Miss Pross enters with a baby, which she kisses and hands to Lucie

Lucie Time passed — and among the advancing echoes there was the tread of a child's feet and the sound of her prattling words. Her husband's step was strong and prosperous among them; her father's firm and equal.

A crackle of thunder. The Light yellows, darkens

Manette But there were other echoes, from a distance, that rumbled menacingly in the corner all through the space of time till now — about young Lucie's sixth birthday. And they began to have an awful sound, as of a great storm in France with a dreadful sea rising.

The music should by now be a variation on the tune that from time to time we have heard Mme Defarge humming to herself. Through the following dialogue it grows more insistent. One or two voices sing along with it. By the interval, the whole company is singing

First Narrator On a night in mid-July, one thousand seven hundred and eighty-nine ...

A flash of lightning. Crack of thunder

Mr Lorry enters, shaking the wet from him

I began to think that I should have to pass the night at Tellson's.
Lucie You are soaked!
Mr Lorry We have been so full of business all day, that we have not known what to do first or which way to turn.
Lucie Tell me.

Act I, Scene 16

Mr Lorry There is such uneasiness in Paris. Our customers over there seem not to be able to confide their property to us fast enough.
Lucie That has a bad look.
Mr Lorry Yes, yes — but we don't know what reason there is in it. People are so unreasonable! Some of us at Tellson's are getting old.
Lucie Still, you know how gloomy and threatening the sky has been all afternoon.

Another crack of thunder. Marching feet in the distance

Mr Lorry I know. I know. But I am determined to be peevish after my long day.

Thunder

(*Anxiously*) Where is Manette?
Dr Manette He is here.
Mr Lorry And Charles? Where is Charles?
Lucie With Lucie ...
Mr Lorry The precious child is safe in bed?

Darnay enters

Darnay And sleeping soundly.
Mr Lorry That's right; all safe and well! I don't know why anything should be otherwise than safe and well here. Thank God. All safe and well ...

A bright, bright flash of lightning followed by a mighty crack of thunder. When it clears, we hear the revolutionary song, loud and clear, sung by the whole company; the family group stand and gaze out fearfully. When the verse finishes, there is a great shout, and Defarge, with a small group of armed citizens "On high fever strain and at high fever heat ... " erupts from the back of the stage. They hurtle forward. The family group scatters. The citizens kneel and take aim out into the audience

Defarge (*yelling over the noise*) Come then! Patriots and friends, we are ready! The Bastille!!

And they fire off a round. Deafening

Black-out

ACT II

Scene 1

The City

Dim light; just a candle. Piano music. Very, very far away, a roar. (A river, a crowd, a battle?)

Sydney Carton alone. Drunk/visionary. A truth before him

Carton When I enter a great city by night I know every one of the houses encloses its own secret; every room in every one of them encloses its own secret. Every heart in the hundreds of thousands is a secret to the heart nearest it. Something of the awfulness of Death is referable to this. Death. Death. The inexorable perpetration of the secret. In any of the burial places of this city is there a sleeper more unknowable than its busy inhabitants are to me, or than I am to them ...?

A beat. Suddenly the roar breaks through. It is a thousand voices chanting

Scene 2

The Bastille

Citizens Death, DEATH, DEATH, DEATH, DEATH.

Carton disappears from sight

A rush of flame across the stage. Smoke, shadows, cries, screams. "Alarm bells ringing, drums beating ... so tremendous was the noise"

First Citizen The White Flag!
Defarge The Bastille has surrendered!

A great cheer and yell

Citizens The prisoners! The records! The secret cells! The instruments of torture.

Act II, Scene 2   55

From the depths comes the Governor of the Bastille with one soldier. They climb upwards

Citizens come down from above and others move upwards after the Governor. Eventually the Citizens catch up with the Governor. Defarge and two Citizens are to one side, Mme Defarge and three others to the other side

Defarge Monsieur the Governor! You are our prisoner.
Governor Rebel dog! You shall pay a terrible price for this.
Defarge A price you shall never live to exact.
Governor Scarecrows and barbarians. The King and his army will crush you as fire burns dry tinder. You are a sickness in the land.
Defarge A sickness from which you shall never recover.

A fight. The soldier is overwhelmed and pinioned. The Governor ends messily skewered by Defarge, then hacked at and stabbed and struck at by the other six. When finally he falls, Mme Defarge kneels over the body, and with a long knife, cuts off the Governor's head. With cries of triumph she and her crew descend, back to the boiling ocean of rebellion down below. Defarge and one Revolutionary, armed with a crowbar and carrying a torch, turn to the soldier

What is the meaning of One Hundred and Five North Tower? Quick!
Soldier (*terrified*) The meaning, Monsieur?
Defarge Is it a captive or a place of captivity? Or do you mean that I shall strike you dead?
Revolutionary Kill him!
Soldier It is a cell!
Defarge Show it me.
Soldier This way ...

They climb up and up, and come to a door

One Hundred and Five North Tower!!
Defarge Open it.

The Soldier turns a key. Defarge and the Revolutionary go in. The noise reduces to a deep, hoarse roar

Revolutionary Empty!
Defarge Good. Pass that torch along these walls, that I may see them. (*Searching the wall*) Stop! Look there.

Revolutionary (*looking*) "A.M.'
Defarge "Alexandre Manette'. Give me that crowbar. (*And he ducks into a corner, wrenching at the floorboards, skirting, whatever. After a few moments, a cry of triumph*) I have it! I have it! I knew it would be here.
Revolutionary Some treasure, citizen?
Defarge Only a paper, citizen. Only a written paper. But treasure of a kind!

The Lights go out on them

Three Citizens, dressed in ragged revolutionary garb, dusty and covered in blood, advance on the audience. Each has a pole and at the end of each pole, a head. As each speaks, he lowers the head, and a Fourth Citizen, in a great black cloak, jams the head on to a spike sticking up from behind masking. As he moves on, each "dead head" should become an actor's head: Aristocrats One, Two and Three. The trick has been worked by virtue of the Fourth Citizen's all-concealing cloak. Rising music

First Citizen The sea rushed on. The remorseless sea of destruction, turbulently swaying shapes, voices of vengeance and faces hardened in the grimaces of suffering.
Second Citizen I know how hard it has grown for me, the wearer of this, to support life in myself, but do you know how easy it has grown for me, the wearer of this, to destroy life in you?
Third Citizen Fierce figures were steadily wending east, west, north and south. Fortified towns, guard houses, gates, trenches and drawbridges were so much air against them. Wheresoever they went, the rising sun found the bodies of men hanging across once peaceful streets, and fires burning.
Fourth Citizen (*turning from his third "head"*) In such risings of fire and risings of sea, the firm earth shaken by the rules of an angry ocean which had now no ebb, *four years of tempest* were consumed.

SCENE 3

Tellson's

The music reaches crescendo. The Light focuses down on to the three heads. A moment of silence, and suddenly they walk free from behind the masking: three exiled Aristocrats, émigrés. Down swings a sign for Tellson's Bank

First Aristo My castle burned!
Second Aristo My horses roasted!
Third Aristo My coaches burnt for firewood!
First Aristo We are no longer appreciated as a class!

Act II, Scene 3   57

Third Aristo (*hushed*) The King is dead.
Second Aristo (*indignant*) He owed me 40,000 livres!
First Aristo He owed me 80,000!
Third Aristo (*to the First*) You owe me as much!
First Aristo (*to the Second*) And you owe me a great deal more!

Mr Lorry bustles in with Darnay

And you, gentlemen — owe Tellson's several hundred thousand between you.
First Aristo When the rebellion is suppressed ——
Second Aristo And the monarchy restored ——
Third Aristo And our estates returned to us ...
Darnay By whom?

A beat

First Aristo What?
Darnay What power can turn this tide now? Would you do battle with the wind and waves?
First Aristo (*hastily*) We have friends and allies, sir, in every country in Europe.
Second Aristo Our friends have armies!
Third Aristo There is a great plan.
First Aristo A secret plan. I have a letter from the King's brother ...
Mr Lorry And I have an urgent letter for a gentleman — a French gentleman, supposedly in England. I have referred it to every client of ours, and no-one can tell me where this gentleman is to be found.
Second Aristo His name?
Mr Lorry The Marquis St Evrémonde.
First Aristo *Morbleu!*
Third Aristo Decadent!
First Aristo Traitor!
Second Aristo Degenerate nephew of the Marquis who was murdered.
Third Aristo Happy to say — never knew him.
Second Aristo A craven who abandoned his post.
First Aristo Infected with the new doctrines; abandoned his estates, left them to the ruffian herd.
Darnay You may not understand the gentleman.
First Aristo Damn the fellow.
Darnay I know the fellow ...
First Aristo I am sorry for it.
Darnay Why?
First Aristo There is contamination in such a scoundrel.

Second Aristo I wonder he is not at the head of the mob.
First Aristo No, no, gentlemen. I know a little of human nature. This fellow would never trust himself to the mercies of his vulgar protégés. No. He'll turn his back on them early in the engagement, and sneak away.
Darnay (*stung*) I tell you ...!

But the Aristocrats move away

Mr Lorry Will you take charge of the letter? You know where to deliver it?
Darnay I do.

And the scene breaks up. Darnay opens the letter

SCENE 4

Gabelle

Narrator Very ill at ease with himself, and with these noble emigrants and with most other men — Darnay made his way into the street, opened the letter and read it.
Darnay (*appalled*) It is from Gabelle!

Immediate switch of scene

Gabelle is thrown on. Two citizen Red Caps interrogate him

First Red Cap You are accused of acting against the people for an emigrant, an aristocrat — Charles Evrémonde.
Second Red Cap Citizen Gabelle, you will await your trial in the prison of the Abbaye in Paris.
Gabelle In the name of liberty, in the name of brotherhood! I have always acted for the people. Charles Evrémonde forsook his inheritance; left instructions, orders, that I was to help the people. He is a friend, a comrade of the people.
First Red Cap Then why does he hide in England, Citizen Gabelle? His place is surely at our side.
Second Red Cap If he so loves the people, how can he bear a moment's absence from their company?
Gabelle I have repaid the taxes, I have collected no rent, I have imposed no fines ...
First Red Cap (*with finality*) You have acted for an emigrant. Your life is forfeit.

And the Red Caps leave

The Light goes tight in on Gabelle

Act II, Scene 5

Gabelle (*out front*) For the love of heaven, of justice, of generosity, of the honour of your noble name, I supplicate you, dear Monsieur, to succour and release me. For the sake of our old friendship, in the name of your dear mother, I pray you, be true to me.

Darnay turns to Gabelle, but he is gone from sight

Darnay (*momentarily in agony*) Gabelle, Gabelle! My good and faithful friend! I would have been there, would have found a way to come, to supervise the change *myself*. I have been unkind, thoughtless, slow to act.

SCENE 5

Departure

Lucie joins Darnay

Lucie Charles?
Darnay Oh my love, I have heard such news. My country cries out, fire lights fire, the innocent are slain for standing in the shadows of the guilty ...
Lucie But you do so much already. We have helped a dozen fugitives, written a thousand letters, sought to protect old friends ...
Darnay But always from a distance. I have acted selfishly, imperfectly ...
Lucie You have been faithful to your family. I know what it has cost ...
Darnay Too little.
Lucie I beg you, Charles, do not be tempted back.
Darnay I could help; speak for mercy and humanity, rescue an old friend ...
Lucie I know that if you return to France I shall never see you again. It is a fine and worthy thing to plunge into the torrent when a man is drowning, but madness to do it when the rescuer will die as certainly as he who would be rescued. You cannot throw your life away, Charles Darnay. Think of your daughter, think of our life together.
Darnay Yes, yes of course. My love ...

And they embrace

Lucie smiles and goes

Music: restless, sinister

First Narrator But his resolution was made. He must go to Paris.
Second Narrator The Lodestone Rock was drawing him, and he must sail on until he struck.
First Narrator But he knew of no rock, he saw hardly any danger.

Darnay (*enthusiastically*) His good intentions to the people, the reforms on his estate, presented themselves before him in an aspect that would be gratefully acknowledged in France on his presenting himself to assert them.

First Narrator Urgent business of Tellson's Bank called Mr Lorry to Paris.

Mr Lorry advances to Darnay with valise and bag

Mr Lorry It is safe enough for me: nobody will care to interfere with an old fellow of hard upon four score when there are so many people there much better worth interfering with.

Darnay I have delivered that letter. Will you take a verbal answer?

Mr Lorry That I will, and readily.

Darnay It is to a prisoner in the Abbaye.

Mr Lorry His name?

Darnay Gabelle. Say simply: he has received the letter and will come.

Mr Lorry Any time mentioned?

Darnay He will start upon his journey tomorrow night!

Mr Lorry I shall say so. Well, goodbye dear fellow. My love to Lucie and to little Lucie — and take precious care of them till I come back.

They shake hands

Lorry turns and goes

Darnay looks guiltily away

Darnay That night he sat up late and wrote two letters: one to Lucie explaining the strong obligation he was under to go to Paris, the other to the Doctor, confiding Lucie and their dear child to his care.

First Narrator The next evening he embraced Lucie, pretending that he would return by and by, and emerged into the heavy mist of the heavy street, with a heavier heart.

Narrators bring him coat, hat, bag

Gabelle appears, high up, way back

Gabelle For the love of heaven, of justice, of generosity, of the honour of your noble name, I supplicate you, dear Monsieur, to succour and release me.

And Darnay turns and moves swiftly away

Act II, Scene 6

At once a change of Light. Distant drumming. Off stage a hard knocking. When it stops——

Scene 6

Place du Carrousel

First Narrator Tellson's Bank, established near the Place du Carrousel in Paris was in the wing of a large house, from the rear windows of which it was possible to glimpse one of the sharper children of the revolution: the guillotine!!

Knock knock knock

Lorry enters, struggling into his jacket

Mr Lorry Thank God that no-one near and dear to me is in this dreadful town today. May He have mercy on all who are in danger ...

He wrestles with a door, pulls back bolts, unlocks it

Lucie and Dr Manette burst in, followed by Miss Pross. All are in coats, with light luggage

Mr Lorry (*astonished*) Manette!
Dr Manette Oh my dear friend ...
Mr Lorry Lucie! What has brought you here? Pross! ... Something is wrong. What has happened?
Lucie It is Charles!
Mr Lorry What of him?
Lucie He is here.
Mr Lorry Here, in Paris?
Lucie Has been here some days — three or four, I don't know how many ... I can't collect my thoughts. An errand of generosity brought him here, unknown to us; he was stopped at the barrier and sent to prison!
Mr Lorry No! *No!*
Dr Manette I fear it is the truth.
Mr Lorry You will be safe here at Tellson's.

They hurry on to other rooms

Defarge and two Red Caps shove Darnay on

Defarge You are consigned, Evrémonde, to the prison of La Force.
Darnay Just heaven! Under what laws, and for what offence?
Defarge We have new laws and new offences since you were here.

Defarge gestures the Red Caps away

Defarge (*in a low voice*) Is it you who married the daughter of Dr Manette, once a prisoner in the Bastille?
Darnay (*surprised*) Yes!
Defarge My name is Defarge.
Darnay (*brightening*) Yes, I remember. My wife came to your home to reclaim her father.
Defarge In the name of our new mistress, La Guillotine, you should not have come to France.
Darnay Indeed — all here is so changed, so sudden and unfair, I feel I am lost. Monsieur Defarge, will you render me a little help?
Defarge I shall do nothing for you. My duty is to my country and the People. I am the sworn servant of both, against you. I will do nothing for you.

And the Red Caps propel Darnay away

Louder drumming. The murmur of a great crowd

Dr Manette returns and gestures at the windows. Mr Lorry and Lucie hurry after

Dr Manette What is that noise?
Mr Lorry Don't look! Manette, for your life — don't look out!
Dr Manette My dear friend, I have a charmed life in this city. I have been a Bastille prisoner. There is no patriot in Paris who would touch me, except to overwhelm me with embraces, or carry me in triumph. My old pain has given me a power that has brought us through the barrier, and gained us news of Charles there, and brought us here.
Lucie We must know the worst, Mr Lorry, whatever our fear.

The drumming gets louder. Cheers, shouts

What is that noise?
Mr Lorry For pity's sake.
Lucie Don't be afraid. Father?

Scene 7

The Guillotine

And Dr Manette opens the windows — whatever. Immediately the sounds become intense. Figures appear all over. Ghoulish puppets peer over ledges

A great guillotine at the rear of the stage moves forward. Behind it, an Executioner, Defarge, a Soldier; at its foot Mme Defarge and another woman, knitting. Cries of "Liberty, fraternity, equality"

Defarge (*calling out*) Condemned by the Tribunal sitting in the First Year of the Republic, the 14th Thermidor, twenty-two enemies of the people. First, Philippe d'Agray, the former Comte de Montauban.

The hapless aristocrat is dragged to the guillotine, his head forced on to the block, and the execution takes place — to a great cheer and roll of drums. The Executioner lifts the head and shows it. (See Production Notes)

Mme Defarge ONE!
Defarge Second. Pierre Verniaud, former member of the National Convention, and counter-revolutionary.

Verniaud is dragged up and executed. His head is shown to the people. A cheer

Mme Defarge TWO!

The scene freezes. A single drum beat

Soldier It sheared off so many, that it and the ground it most polluted were a rotten red.
Bystander It hushed the eloquent, struck down the powerful, abolished the beautiful and good.
Mme Defarge Twenty-two friends of note, twenty-one living and one dead, it lopped the heads off that morning in as many minutes. Traitors, aristocrats, priests, emigrants and enemies of the people!

The guillotine moves back. The Lights come down on the main stage so that the focus shifts to Dr Manette, Lucie and Mr Lorry above

Dr Manette Dr Manette hastened out into the public square when the terrible ritual of death had run its bloody course.

Lucie (*watching*) His streaming white hair, his remarkable face, and the impetuous confidence of his manner, carried him to the heart of the terrible throng.

Mr Lorry And then Mr Lorry saw him in the midst of a dense group, linked shoulder to shoulder, who hurried him away with cries of "Live the Bastille prisoner..."

We hear voices echoing this

"Help for the Bastille prisoner's kindred in La Force! Room for the Bastille prisoner in front here! Save the prisoner Evrémonde at La Force!"

The Lights go down on Dr Manette

Lorry goes

Scene 8

Mme Defarge Pays A Visit

Lucie On the morning of the second day, Dr Manette had still not returned; but Tellson's Bank received another visitor ...

Miss Pross enters behind Mme Defarge, grim and ready for a scrap

Mme Defarge (*impatiently*) Where is Madame Darnay?
Miss Pross Well, I am sure, Boldface! I hope you are pretty well.
Mme Defarge I must see her. If I am to protect her, I must see her.
Miss Pross Ay, ay, gabble away in your devil's hocus-pocus. I'm a good Englishwoman and lucky not to understand.
Mme Defarge Besides I have a note for her.

Lucie arrives from above

Pross Well all I have to say to you is that I am a subject of His Most Gracious Majesty King George the Third (*she curtsies*) and as such, my maxim is, confound your politics, frustrate your knavish tricks, on him our hopes we fix, God Save the King!
Lucie Miss Pross, for heaven's sake. (*To Mme Defarge*) Madame ...?
Mme Defarge Defarge.
Lucie (*startled*) Madame Defarge ... Our good Pross is an English lady and knows no French.
Mme Defarge So you are his child.

Act II, Scene 8

Lucie My father is Dr Manette. My husband ...
Mme Defarge I have a note from him.
Lucie From Charles, from my husband? Oh, good gracious, Pross, I think I shall faint. A letter from Charles, from La Force; Pross, you must read it to me. Here. Tell me what it says.
Miss Pross (*carefully*) Dearest, take courage. I am well, and your father has influence around me. You cannot answer this. Kiss our child for me.
Lucie Thank God, thank God. Madame Defarge, this is a blessing to us.

And Lucie kisses the knitting hands. "But the hands made no response, dropped cold and heavy and took to knitting again." A chilly moment

Mme Defarge It is enough. I have seen you. I must go.
Lucie You will be good to my husband. You will do him no harm. You will help me to see him if you can?
Mme Defarge Your husband is not my business here. It is the daughter of your father who is my business here.
Lucie For my sake, then, be merciful to my husband. For my child's sake. We are more afraid of you than of these others.
Mme Defarge (*with a grim smile*) What does your husband say in his little letter?
Lucie (*nervously*) That my father has much influence around him.
Mme Defarge Surely it will release him! Let it do so.
Lucie (*alarmed*) I implore you not to exercise any power that you possess against my innocent husband. Oh sister-woman, imagine yourself in my place, as a wife and mother.
Mme Defarge (*sharply*) The wives and mothers I have been used to, since I was a child, have not been greatly considered. I have known their husbands and fathers laid in prison and kept from them often enough. All our lives we have seen our sister-women and their children suffer poverty, hunger, misery, oppression and neglect of all kinds. Judge you! Is it likely that the trouble of one wife and mother would be much to us now?

Mme Defarge leaves

Lucie Oh Pross, my courage deserts me.
Miss Pross Oh my Ladybird, it takes courage to say so.
Lucie I am not unhopeful, but that dreadful woman seems to throw a shadow on me and on all my hopes.
Miss Pross Like a great grey cloud, my pet: no substance in it, but frightful to behold.

They hug and smile. A moment of peace. Music

SCENE 9

Fifteen Months

This scene must give the impression of relentless movement back and forth. People meeting briefly, separating, moving on. Snatches of news, moments of conversation, hurried encounters. Music moves this to its climax

Mr Lorry (*hurrying to Dr Manette and shaking his hand*) Dr Manette did not return until the morning of the fourth day of his absence.
Dr Manette (*passing on to Miss Pross and Lucie*) I was taken to the prison of La Force, there presented, by the crowd that took me, to the tribunal. One of the body rose, identified me ...
Defarge (*above and behind, pointing down*) He is the man he says he is.
Dr Manette (*back to Miss Pross and Lucie*) I was greeted with the greatest excitement and managed to persuade the tribunal to send for Charles. He was examined. The President conferred with Defarge, then said:
President (*above, elsewhere*) The prisoner must remain in custody, but for your sake, he shall be held inviolate in safe custody.

Miss Pross and Lucie exit

Mr Lorry (*watching Dr Manette as the women go*) Mr Lorry feared the scenes of carnage, the anxiety, the horror of the time, would presently revive the old danger in his friend. But he need *not* have feared.
Dr Manette (*warmly to Lorry*) My years of desolation were not mere waste and ruin. As my beloved child restored me to myself, I will restore to her the dearest part of herself. By Heaven I will do it!

And he sets off for the cells; during the following he arrives with Darnay

First Narrator All things seemed to yield before his persevering purpose.
Second Narrator He used his influence so wisely that he was soon the respected physician of three prisons, and among them of La Force.
Darnay (*above, with Dr Manette*) He saw Charles Darnay weekly, and took sweet messages to Lucie, straight from his lips.

During the following Dr Manette leaves Darnay in order to meet Lucie

Above, a Member of the Committee of Public Safety

Member (*announcing*) The Republic of Liberty, Equality, Fraternity or death, declared for victory or death against the world in arms ...

Act II, Scene 9

Loud cheers

Dr Manette But though the Doctor tried hard, and never ceased trying, to get Charles Darnay set at liberty or at least to get him brought to trial, the public current of the time had set too strong and fast for him.
First Narrator There was no pause, no pity, no peace, no interval of relenting rest, no measurement of time.
Second Narrator The executioner showed the people the head of the King's wife!
Lucie One year and three months. During all that time, Lucie was never sure, from hour to hour, but that the guillotine would strike off her husband's head next day.
Second Narrator And every day, through the stony streets, the tumbrils jolted heavily, filled with condemned.
First Narrator No pause, no pity, no peace, no interval of relenting rest.
Second Narrator And then, one morning in December ...

Dr Manette arrives by Lucie

Charles is summoned for tomorrow.
Lucie For tomorrow!
Dr Manette There is no time to lose. I am well prepared. Your suspense is nearly ended. He shall be restored to you.

A Judge and Prosecutor appear on an upper level

Judge (*above*) The dread tribunal of judge, public prosecutor and determined jury sat every day ...
Prosecutor (*above*) Charles Evrémonde, called Darnay, you are accused as an emigrant — banished on pain of death.
All TAKE OFF HIS HEAD!
Prosecutor You are not an emigrant?
Darnay No, not in the sense accepted by the tribunal.
Prosecutor But you married in England?
Darnay Yes.
Prosecutor Who?
Darnay Lucie Manette, only daughter of Dr Manette, the good physician who sits there.

Cheers and hubbub

(*Through the cheers*) I have come back, to save a citizen's life, and to bear his testimony, at whatever personal hazard, to the truth. Is that criminal in the eyes of the republic?

All NO! NO!
Dr Manette So far from being in favour with the aristocratic government in England, Charles Darnay has actually been tried for his life by it, as the foe to England, and friend of the United States!

Loud cheers! Tumult

Judge Your verdict, citizens?
All NOT GUILTY!

Applause, shouts. Darnay is lifted up. A jagged piece of the Marseillaise sounds, the tricolour is looped round his neck, with flowers. He is set down next to Lucie

Everyone exits apart from the family group: Miss Pross, Dr Manette, Lucie, Darnay

Euphoria. The Lights change. We are back in Manette's apartment

Darnay Lucie! My own! I am safe!
Lucie My dearest Charles. Thank God, thank God!
Darnay Your father's triumph. No other man in all of France could have done what he has done for me.
Dr Manette Never cry, my dearest, don't tremble so. I have saved him!
Miss Pross May I ask a question, Dr Manette?
Dr Manette I think you may take that liberty ...
Miss Pross For gracious sake, don't talk about liberty, we've had quite enough of that.
Lucie Pross!
Miss Pross Is there any prospect yet of our getting out of this place?
Dr Manette I fear not. It would be dangerous.
Miss Pross Heigh ho hum. Then we must have patience and wait.

Laughter. A sound. Lucie cries out. Sudden silence

Lucie What is that?
Dr Manette My dear!
Lucie I thought I heard a sound upon the stairs.
Dr Manette My love, the staircase is as still as death.

A long prickly silence. Then, with maximum clatter, a door bursts open. Three men in red caps enter

First Red Cap The Citizen Evrémonde, called Darnay!
Second Red Cap I know you, Evrémonde. I saw you at the tribunal today. You are again the prisoner of the Republic.

Act II, Scene 10

Lucie screams. Another silence

Dr Manette (*quietly*) How does this happen?
First Red Cap He has been denounced to the section of Saint Antoine.
Dr Manette Who has denounced him?
Second Red Cap It is against the rule ——
Dr Manette Who has denounced him?
First Red Cap He is denounced — and gravely — by the Citizen and Citizeness Defarge. And by one other.
Dr Manette By what other?
First Red Cap Do you ask, Citizen Doctor?
Dr Manette Yes.
First Red Cap (*after a moment*) Then you will be answered tomorrow. Come.

Darnay is hurried out

Lucie turns to Dr Manette. Despair is written on his face

Unable to comfort her, Dr Manette turns and goes

The Lights fade. A bell tolls

Scene 10

An Encounter

Sydney Carton, once again in the light of a street lamp. He is half away from us, lunging at a distance. A figure — Mr Barsad — moves

Carton (*calling*) Mr Barsad! A word with you.

A moment, and Mr Barsad comes clattering down; stops, stares, still at a distance

Carton I lighted on you, Mr Barsad, coming out of the prison of the Conciergerie an hour or more ago. I have been following you, Mr Barsad.
Barsad That's not my name.
Carton Why do you answer to it then?
Barsad Who the devil are you?
Carton A stranger. One who remembers a face well. We have not seen you at the Old Bailey for a while.
Barsad What's your meaning?

Carton Trial of Charles Darnay. For treason. You were a witness, Mr Barsad. Having this reason for associating you with the misfortunes of my friend, now very unfortunate, I walked in your direction. And, gradually, what I had done at random, seemed to shape itself into a purpose, Mr Barsad.
Barsad What purpose?
Carton It would be troublesome and might be dangerous to you if I explained it in the street. I am staying at Tellson's with Mr Jarvis Lorry. I only arrived there yesterday evening. Perhaps you could show me the quickest way ...?
Barsad Under a threat?
Carton Oh! Did I say that?
Barsad Then why should I go with you?
Carton Really Mr Barsad, I can't say if you can't.
Barsad Do you mean that you won't say, sir?
Carton You apprehend me very clearly, Mr Barsad. I won't.

A moment. Barsad is nervous

Barsad I'll hear what you have to say. Yes. I'll go with you.

Scene 11

Prison

Carton and Barsad turn and go

A clanging door. Charles Darnay caught in a narrow shaft of light, a pattern of prison bars. Round him, cries, sobs. The Seamstress at a distance from him, by a guttering candle

Darnay (*incoherently*) Now am I left — as if I were dead ... five paces by four and a half, five paces by four and a half, five paces by four and a half ... he made shoes, but lived ... and there among the ghosts in the other room ... she stood, she was there, a woman like her, a gleam of candlelight on her hair ... she looked like ... No ... five paces by four and a half, five paces by four and a half ... How could she be here ... HOW COULD SHE BE HERE?

The clang of a prison door. Another door bangs

Darnay and the Seamstress vanish from sight

A warm fire crackles and glows. Carton, Barsad with Mr Lorry

SCENE 12

A Hand at Cards

Carton (*to Lorry*) Mr Barsad is a spy. A spy within the prisons here.
Mr Lorry Barsad? Barsad? I know that name.
Carton The Old Bailey. Witness at the trial.
Mr Lorry Great heavens yes! I hoped I might never set eyes on you again, sir.
Carton And will wish you hadn't now. I followed him, listened to his conversation. Darnay has been arrested again.
Mr Lorry (*horrified*) What do you tell me?! I left him safe and free within these two hours.
Carton Mr Barsad took the soldiers to Charles Darnay's door. When was it done, Mr Barsad?
Barsad An hour ago.
Carton And he will go before the tribunal of Saint Antoine tomorrow?
Barsad I believe so.
Mr Lorry But surely Dr Manette could have prevented this arrest.
Carton I own to you, Mr Lorry, I am shaken that he could not. But perhaps his influence may stand Darnay in as good stead tomorrow as today ...
Mr Lorry (*doubtfully*) Perhaps ...
Carton But this is a desperate time, when desperate games are played for desperate stakes. Let the Doctor play the winning game; I will play the losing one. The stake I have resolved to play for — in case of the worst — is a friend at the Conciergerie. That friend is you, Mr Barsad ...
Barsad You need have good cards, sir.
Carton I'll run them over. I'll see what I hold.

Carton turns to Mr Lorry

Mr Lorry, you know what a brute I am. I wish you'd give me a little brandy.

Wondering, Mr Lorry obliges. After a moment ...

Mr Barsad, Emissary of republican committees, now turnkey, now prisoner, always spy and secret informer, represents himself to his latest employers under a false name. That's a very good card. Mr Barsad, now in the employ of the republican French government, was formerly in the employ of the aristocratic English government, the enemy of France and freedom. That's an excellent card. Inference clear as day that Mr Barsad is the spy of Pitt; an English traitor, and agent of so much mischief spoken of and so difficult to find. That's my card not to be beaten. Have you followed my hand, Mr Barsad?

Barsad *(very uneasy)* Not to understand your play.

Carton I play my ace: denunciation of Mr Barsad to the nearest section committee. Look over your hand, Mr Barsad, and see what you have. Don't hurry. *(He turns, pours himself a drink)*

Barsad stares nervously into the fire. Mr Lorry watches him

You scarcely seem to like your hand.

Barsad *(to Lorry)* I think, sir, I may appeal to a gentleman of your years and benevolence, whether this other gentleman can under any circumstances reconcile it to his station to play that ace of which he has spoken ...

Carton *(sharply)* I play my ace, Mr Barsad, without any scruple, in a very few minutes.

A long moment

Barsad You told me of a proposal. What is it? Now, it is of no use asking too much of me. We are all desperate here. I may denounce you if I think proper. What do you want?

Carton Not very much. You are a turnkey at the Conciergerie?

Barsad I tell you once and for all, there is no such thing as escape possible ...

Carton Why need you tell me what I have not asked? You are a turnkey?

Barsad I am sometimes.

Carton You can be when you choose.

Barsad I can pass in and out when I choose.

Carton Very well. You will escort me in to see our prisoner when the time is right.

Barsad *(reluctantly)* It could be done.

Carton It must be.

Barsad Will be then ...

Carton We shall meet tomorrow night if needs be, after the trial. There will be other details to explain ... Good-night, Mr Barsad. And thank you.

Barsad is about to speak, thinks better of it. He goes

Mr Lorry But access to him will not save him.

Carton I never said it would.

Mr Lorry turns away, tears in his eyes

Act II, Scene 12   73

You are a good man and a true friend. Forgive me if I notice that you are affected. I could not see my father weep and sit by, careless. And I could not respect your sorrow more if you were my father. You are free from that misfortune, however.

Mr Lorry looks up, surprised, and gives Carton his hand

Don't tell Lucie of this arrangement with Mr Barsad. It would not enable her to go and see poor Darnay. I shall not see her. I can help her without that. (*Beat*) How does she look?
Mr Lorry Anxious and unhappy but very beautiful.
Carton (*a long grieving sound, like a sigh — almost a sob*) Ah!
Mr Lorry (*concerned*) Mr Carton!
Carton (*turning the subject*) And your duties here have drawn to an end?
Mr Lorry Yes. I have my leave to pass. I was ready to go.

A moment

Carton Yours is a long life to look back upon.
Mr Lorry I am in my seventy-eighth year.
Carton You have been useful all your life; steadily occupied, trusted, respected.
Mr Lorry I have been a man of business ever since I have been a man. Indeed I may say that I was a man of business when a boy!
Carton See what a place you fill at seventy-eight. How many people will miss you when you leave it empty.
Mr Lorry A solitary old bachelor. Nobody will weep for me.
Carton How can you say that? Wouldn't she weep for you? Wouldn't her child?
Mr Lorry Yes, yes, thank God. I didn't quite mean what I said.
Carton It is a thing to thank God for; is it not?
Mr Lorry Surely, surely.
Carton Tell me: does your childhood seem far off?
Mr Lorry No. For as I draw closer and closer to the end, I travel in the circle, nearer and nearer to the beginning. My heart is touched now by many remembrances of my pretty little mother and of the days when what we call the world was not so real for me, and my faults were not confirmed in me.
Carton I understand the feeling! And you are the better for it?
Mr Lorry I hope so. But you — you are young.
Carton Yes. But my young way was never the way of age. (*Beat*) Enough of me.

Mr Lorry And of me I am sure.
Carton Good-night. I shall prowl the streets awhile. But never fear, I shall see you at the court in the morning Good-night.
Mr Lorry Good-night.

SCENE 13

The Chemist's Shop

First Narrator Sydney Carton went out into the street. Under a glimmering lamp, he wrote with a pencil on a scrap of paper.
Second Narrator Then, traversing — with the decided step of one who remembered the way well — several dark and dirty streets, he stopped at a chemist's shop.
Carton Good-night, citizen.
Chemist Good-night to you.
Carton (*handing the scrap of paper*) You can supply me.
Chemist (*reading*) Whew! (*A moment*) For you, citizen?
Carton For me.
Chemist You will be careful to keep them separate, citizen? You know the consequences of mixing them?
Carton Perfectly.

The Chemist withdraws for a moment

Music plays. Carton's theme perhaps. Haunting, sad

There is nothing more to do — until tomorrow.

The Chemist returns with three small packets

Carton pays the Chemist, pockets the drugs. There are figures lying, sitting, sleeping under dark cloaks. All in position to spring up as the revolutionary court

There is nothing more to do. I can't sleep.

The Lights focus down on to Carton. The Narrator who speaks now could be Lorry

Narrator Long ago, as a youth of great promise, he had followed his father to his grave. His mother had died years before. These words, read at his father's grave, arose now in his mind ...

Act II, Scene 14   75

Carton I am the resurrection and the life, sayeth the Lord: he that believeth in me, though he were dead, yet shall he live; and whosoever liveth and believeth in me *shall never die ...*
Narrator His was the settled manner of a tired man, who had wandered and struggled and got lost but who at length struck into his road and saw its end.

Carton stares, sighs, smiles a little. Turns on his heel and walks away. A beat.

Scene 14

The Tribunal of St Antoine

Bright Light suddenly, and the roar of a crowd. The sleeping figures cast off their cloaks. Tattered red caps, dirty suits, "life-thrusting, cannibal-looking, bloody-minded" citizens. A President on high, a Prosecutor. Darnay in the dock. Lorry and Dr Manette facing Defarge and Mme Defarge

Prosecutor Charles Evrémonde, called Darnay! Released yesterday. Re-accused and re-taken yesterday. Suspected and denounced enemy of the Republic, aristocrat, last of a family of tyrants who had used their abolished privileges to the infamous oppression of the people. Under this proscription, the people demand the law upon his head!
President Is the accused openly denounced or secretly?
Prosecutor Openly.
President By whom?
Prosecutor Three voices. Ernest Defarge, wine vendor of Saint Antoine.
President Good.
Prosecutor Thérèse Defarge, his wife.
President Good.
Prosecutor Alexandre Manette, physician.

Uproar. Dr Manette

Dr Manette (*springing to his feet; outraged*) Who and where is the false conspirator, who says that I denounce the husband of my child!
President Citizen Manette, be tranquil. Listen to what is to follow. Be silent!
Prosecutor Citizen Defarge!

And the Citizen stands

You did good service at the taking of the Bastille, citizen.
Defarge So they say ...
Prosecutor Inform the Tribunal of what you did that day within the Bastille.

Defarge I knew that this doctor who I used to serve had been confined in a cell known as One Hundred and Five North Tower. I knew it from himself. I mount to the cell, and search it. Concealed there, I find a written paper. This is that written paper. It is the writing of Dr Manette ...

Prosecutor What does it say, citizen?

Defarge It tells how the prisoner's father and his uncle took the doctor here to see a girl, a peasant girl, abducted by the prisoner's father, violated by the prisoner's father, robbed of her reason by the prisoner's father. It tells of her father's death and of her husband's — her father broken by shame and grief, her husband sacrificed when he refused the prisoner's father his indulgence with the girl. It tells of her brother, murdered when he tried to rescue her. It tells of her death, and how they laughed to be rid of her. It tells how the doctor saw and heard too much, and how they brought him to his living grave. It ends: (*and he flourishes the papers at Darnay; reading*) "These men and their descendants, to the last of their race, I, Alexander Manette, unhappy prisoner do this night in my unbearable agony, denounce to the times when all these things shall be answered for. I denounce them to heaven and to earth!"

Mme Defarge leaps to her feet, blazing, furious

Mme Defarge I smite this bosom with these two hands and I tell you, citizen: that peasant family so injured by the two Evrémonde brothers is my family. That sister of the murdered boy was my sister, that husband was my sister's husband, that brother was my brother, that father was my father, those dead are my dead, and that summons to answer for those things descends to me!!

A great cry goes up

Citizens Guilty! GUILTY! GUILTY!

President Unanimously voted. At heart and by descent an aristocrat, an enemy of the Republic, a notorious oppressor of the people. Convey him to his prison. We pronounce this sentence: Death in four and twenty hours!!

Great cheer

Prosecutor and President go

Red Caps seize Darnay. Mme Defarge intercepts Lucie and Dr Manette on their way to Darnay

Act II, Scene 15

Mme Defarge I have observed your face, Citizen Doctor, I have observed your face to be not the face of a true friend of the Republic. And I have observed your daughter too. Let me but lift my finger ...

And she is gone

Scene 15

Partings

Darnay (*to Lucie*) Farewell — dear darling of my soul.
Lucie I can bear it, dear Charles. A parting blessing for our child.
Darnay I sent it to her by you. I kiss her by you. I say farewell to her by you.

The Red Caps start to move Darnay away

Lucie My husband. No! A moment! We shall not be separated long. I feel that this will break my heart by and by.
Dr Manette (*in tears*) I could have done more, written to a hundred more, hammered at a thousand gates.
Darnay No, no! What have you done, what have you done that you should blame yourself! We know now what you underwent when you suspected my descent, and when you knew it. We thank you with all our hearts, with all our love and duty. Heaven be with you. Heaven be with you both.

And he is led off stage

Lucie swoons. From the remains of the courtroom crowd a ghost rises up: the peasant boy, pale and bloody. He kneels by Lucie and addresses Dr Manette

Boy Doctor! You are my witness. In the days when all these things are to be answered for. *You are my witness.* (*And he melts away, back into the crowd*)
Carton (*stepping forward*) Dr Manette, take her home, look after her, don't recall her to herself. She is better so. Mr Lorry, a word.

Dr Manette carries Lucie away

Mr Lorry (*deeply upset*) All is lost! He will perish.
Carton They are in great danger. They are in danger of denunciation by Madame Defarge. I overheard words of that woman before the start of the

tribunal. She intends her denunciation within the week. The pretence will be the usual one — a prison plot. Don't look so horrified! You will save them all.
Mr Lorry Heaven grant I may, Carton! But how?
Carton You have money and can buy the means of travelling to the sea-coast as quickly as the journey can be made. Have your horses ready so that they're in starting trim at nine o'clock in the morning. For the sake of her child and her father, press upon her the necessity of leaving Paris with them and you at that hour. The moment I come to you, take me in and drive away.
Mr Lorry I understand that I wait for you under all circumstances.
Carton Wait for nothing but to have my place occupied, and then — for England!
Mr Lorry Why then it does not all depend on one old man, but I shall have a young and ardent man at my side.
Carton God willing. Promise me not to change a detail of this plan.
Mr Lorry I promise. And I hope to do my part faithfully.
Carton As I hope to do mine. Now goodbye.
Mr Lorry Goodbye, dear Mr Carton. Until tomorrow.
Carton Adieu.

They shake hands. Mr Lorry hurries out

Carton turns to a figure loitering in the background

Now, Mr Barsad ...

Scene 16

The Conciergerie

And the Lights darken to prison gloom. The bell strikes

First Narrator In the black prison of the Conciergerie, the doomed of the day awaited their fate.
Second Narrator Charles Darnay, alone in a cell, fully comprehended that no personal influence could possibly save him.
First Narrator But it was not easy, with the face of his beloved wife fresh before him, to compose his mind to what it must bear.
Darnay His hold on life was strong, and it was very, very hard to loosen. By gradual efforts and degrees unclosed a little here, it clenched the tighter there; and when he brought his strength to bear on that hand and it yielded, this was closed again.

Act II, Scene 16

First Narrator He wrote a long letter to Lucie, another to her father, a third to Mr Lorry, explaining, entreating, consoling, encouraging. He never thought of Carton. His mind was so full of the others, that he never once thought of him ...

Bells toll during the following

Darnay Nine o'clock in the sombre morning. Gone for ever. The final hour is ten. There is but another now.
Narrator He had never seen the instrument that was to terminate his life.
Darnay (*restless*) How high is it? ... How many steps? ... Where shall I be stood? ... How touched? ... Will their hands be red? ... Which way will they turn my face? ... Will I be the first or last? ...

Suddenly echoing footsteps sound in the silence. The sound of a key in a lock, a door creaking open. We hear Barsad whisper

Barsad Go you in alone; I wait near. Lose no time!

Carton emerges into the light

Carton Of all the people upon earth, you least expected to see me?
Darnay (*amazed*) I cannot believe it to be you! You are not a prisoner?
Carton No. I have some power over one of the keepers here. I bring you a request from her — your wife, dear Darnay.
Darnay What is it?
Carton A most, earnest, pressing and emphatic entreaty. You must comply with it. Take off those boots you wear, and draw on these of mine. Put your hands to them; put your will to them. Quick!
Darnay There is no escaping from this place. It is madness.
Carton Change that cravat for this of mine, that coat for this. Let me take the ribbon from your hair, and shake out your hair like this of mine.
Darnay It cannot be accomplished. It never can be done.
Carton Do I ask you to pass the door? When I ask that — refuse. Here are pen and ink; now, is your hand steady enough to write?
Darnay Yes, yes ...
Carton Write down what I dictate. Quick, friend, quick!!
Darnay To whom do I address it?
Carton To no-one. Listen and write ... (*He dictates; during the following, he takes a bottle and a cloth from his pocket*) If you remember the words that passed between us, long ago, you will readily comprehend this when you see it. You do remember them, I know. It is not in your nature to forget them.

Darnay suddenly looks up. Carton hides the bottle

Have you written "forget them"?
Darnay I have. Is that a weapon in your hand?
Carton No. I am not armed.
Darnay What is it in your hand?
Carton (*urgently*) You shall know directly. Write on; there are but a few words more. (*Dictating; during this speech he empties the contents of the bottle into the cloth*) I am thankful that the time has come when I can prove them. That I do so is no subject for regret or grief. (*He holds the cloth by Darnay's shoulder*)
Darnay What vapour is that?
Carton Vapour?
Darnay Something that crossed me ...
Carton I am conscious of nothing. Take up the pen and finish. Hurry, hurry!
Darnay I feel suddenly faint.
Carton Hurry, Darnay. Rally your attention.
Darnay Yes ...
Carton (*dictating*) If it had been otherwise ...

Darnay seems on the point of collapse

If it had been otherwise ...

Darnay staggers to his feet. Carton leaps forward and presses the cloth to his face. Darnay struggles for a moment, but then loses consciousness. Carton completes the change of clothing. He goes to the door and calls

Carton (*calling*) Enter there! Come in!

Barsad appears

Carton kneels by Darnay, and tucks the note he dictated into his pocket

(*To Barsad*) You see? Is your hazard very great? Now ... get assistance, and take me to the coach.
Barsad You?
Carton Him, man, with whom I have exchanged. You go out by the gate by which you brought me in?
Barsad Of course.
Carton I was weak and faint when you brought me in and I am fainter now you take me out. The parting interview has overpowered me. Quick, call assistance.
Barsad You swear not to betray me?

Act II, Scene 16

Carton (*impatient*) I have sworn. Take him to Mr Lorry as we have arranged. Tell Mr Lorry to remember my words of last night, and drive like the devil.
Barsad (*at the door*) You there! Now.

A Gaoler enters

The prisoner's friend is overcome. Get him out of here. (*To Carton*) The time is short Evrémonde.
Carton I know it well. Be careful of my friend, I entreat you.
Barsad Come then citizen. Lift him with me, and come away.

Barsad and the Gaoler exit with Darnay

The door crashes to. Distant footsteps. Silence. Then the bell begins to toll ten o'clock. Suspense builds. A moment after the tenth stroke, the sound of doors being banged open. One, two, three, four and the fifth is the door of Darnay's cell

Another gaoler enters

Gaoler Come, citizen. It is time.

The Lights change

Other figures gather around Carton. Cloaks, hoods. All the company except the Gaoler, Miss Pross, Mme Defarge. One of the figures muttering a prayer. One of them is the little Seamstress. She comes to him

Seamstress Citizen Evrémonde. I was with you in La Force.
Carton True. I forget what you were accused of.
Seamstress Plots. Though the just heaven knows I am innocent of any. I am a seamstress. Who would think of plotting with me?
Carton Yes.
Seamstress I am not afraid to die, Citizen Evrémonde, if the Republic will profit by my death. But I do not know how that can be.
Carton Nor I.
Seamstress If I may ride with you, Citizen Evrémonde, will you let me hold your hand? It will give me courage. (*She looks up at him, gasps*)

He puts his finger to her lips

Are you dying for him?
Carton And his wife and child. Yes.
Seamstress Oh you will let me hold your brave hand, stranger.
Carton Yes, my poor sister, to the last.

The Lights focus on one cloaked figure. The sound of galloping horses, grinding wheels. The figure is Mr Lorry

Mr Lorry (*disbelieving, amazed*) The wind is rushing after us, and the clouds are flying after us, and the whole wild night is in pursuit of us; but so far, we are pursued by nothing else!

Scene 17

A Duel

And a whirl of light, and we see the figure of Miss Pross standing before a closed door, bags on either side of her. Mme Defarge, a pistol and a long cruel knife in her belt, faces her. Miss Pross screams

Mme Defarge The wife of Evrémonde; where is she?

Miss Pross You might from your appearance be the wife of Lucifer, nevertheless, you shall not get the better of me. I am an Englishwoman!

Mme Defarge I am due at the day's entertainment. They reserve my chair and my knitting for me. I wish to see the wife of Evrémonde.

Miss Pross If those eyes of yours were bed-winches, and I was an English four-poster, they shouldn't loosen a splinter of me. No, you wicked, foreign woman, I am your match.

Mme Defarge Woman, imbecile and pig-like. Stand from the door and let me go to her.

Miss Pross I little thought that I should ever want to understand your language, but I would give all I have to know if you suspect the truth ...

Mme Defarge (*calling*) Citizen doctor! Wife of Evrémonde! Any person but this miserable fool, answer the Citizeness Defarge!

Miss Pross The longer I keep you here, the greater is the hope for my Ladybird.

Mme Defarge If they are gone, they can be pursued and brought back.

Miss Pross I pray for bodily strength to keep you here, while every minute you are here is worth a hundred thousand guineas to my darling.

Mme Defarge Out of my way, wretch! (*And she heads for the door*)

Miss Pross seizes her round the waist and holds her tight. A big struggle. Mme Defarge strikes out. Miss Pross "clasped her tight, and even lifted her from the floor!" Mme Defarge tries to get at her gun

Miss Pross You shall not draw it! I am stronger than you, I bless heaven for it. I'll hold you till one or other of us faints or dies.

Renewed struggle. The gun is free. A flash, a crash, and Mme Defarge falls lifeless to the ground

Act II, Scene 18

A great silence ... a great silence ... a silence fixed and unchangeable ... never to be broken ... never to be broken as long as my life lasts.

SCENE 18

A Far, Far Better Thing

And the Lights go, and the smoke from the pistol grows and swirls round the figures of Carton and the Seamstress on the platform. The shape of the guillotine is close by, half-obliterated by smoke

Executioner The Curé Bernard Finville, traitor to the people.

The sound of the blade dropping. Cheers and shouts

Seamstress I think you were sent to me by heaven.
Carton Or you to me. Keep your eyes upon me child, and mind no other object.
Seamstress I mind nothing while I hold your hand. I shall mind nothing when I let it go, if they are rapid.
Carton They will be rapid. Fear not!
Seamstress I have a cousin whom I love dearly. Tell me, brave friend, will it seem very long while I wait for her in the better land where I am going now?
Carton It cannot be. There is no time there and no trouble.

A beat

Seamstress Am I to kiss you now? Is the moment come?
Carton Yes.

They kiss; she turns away from him and moves out of sight to the guillotine

Executioner Madeleine Buzan, conspirator and traitor to the people!

The blade drops. Then silence. Just the sound of wind blowing

Carton (*looking out*) I see Barsad and Defarge, the juryman, the judge, long ranks of the new oppressors who have risen on the destruction of the old, perishing by this retributive blade before it shall cease out of its present use. I see a beautiful city and a brilliant people rising from the abyss, and in their struggles to be truly free, in their triumphs and defeats, through long years to come, I see the evil of this time and of the time before gradually making expiation for itself and wearing out.

Quiet music: Carton's theme

I see the lives for which I lay down my life, peaceful, useful, prosperous and happy in that England which I shall see no more. I see her with a child upon her bosom, who bears my name. I see that I hold a sanctuary in their hearts, and in the hearts of their descendants, generation upon generation. It is a far, far better thing that I do, than I have ever done; it is a far, far better rest that I go to than I have ever known.

The Light burns brighter and brighter upon him. The music rises to a crescendo. The blade falls, the Lights snap out and the music cuts out sharply, leaving the sound of a cold wind

THE END

FURNITURE AND PROPERTY LIST

ACT I

Ten lanterns
Low bench
Dr Manette: shoemaking tools and lady's shoe
Boy: old sword
First Man and **Second Man**: swords
Mme Defarge: knitting
Workbench
Judge: gavel
"Dead bodies" on ropes
Judge's bench
Table. *On it*: papers, briefs, books
Inn furniture
Glasses of wine
Mirror
Desk. *On it*: books, pile of papers
Armchair
Bottles
Glasses
Basin of water
Towels
Wine shop sign
Large rag dolls
Coin
Table. *On it*: dinner things
Lucie: jug of water, bottle of wine
Heavily laden table
Marquis: snuff box
Pross and **Lorry**: confetti
Book
Pross: baby
Citizens: guns, knives

ACT II

Candle
Mme Defarge: long knife
Revolutionary: crowbar, torch

Soldier: key
Three Citizens: poles with heads attached
Mr Lorry: letter
Mr Lorry: valise, bag
Narrators: coat, hat, bag
Lucie, Dr Manette, Pross: light luggage
Ghoulish puppets
Guillotine, basket, heads (*See* Production Notes)
Tricolour
Flowers
Chemist: three small packets of drugs
Carton: bottle and cloth
Darnay's writing materials
Pross: bags
Mme Defarge: pistol, long knife

LIGHTING PLOT

Practical fittings required: lanterns, street lamp
Composite set. Various interior and exterior settings

ACT I

To open: Darkness

Cue 1	Match is struck *Snap on practical lanterns with covering light*	(Page 1)
Cue 2	Figures scatter *Snap off practicals; bring up fireglow and dim interior lighting*	(Page 2)
Cue 3	**Mr Lorry**: "... and silently disappeared ..." *Lights lower on* **Mr Lorry** *and* **Lucie** *but stay on* **Dr Manette**	(Page 4)
Cue 4	The **Noblemen** stare at **Dr Manette** *Lights fade*	(Page 7)
Cue 5	Music fades *Fireglow and dim interior lighting*	(Page 7)
Cue 6	**Pross**: "... cast my lot in an island?!" *Lights change*	(Page 8)
Cue 7	**Voice**: "You know that you are recalled to life?" *Cross-fade to wine-shop*	(Page 9)
Cue 8	Journey sounds die away. Beat. Silence *Cross-fade to street lighting with street lamp on*	(Page 13)
Cue 9	**Judge**: "Five years later!" *Lights come up dimly on court*	(Page 14)
Cue 10	Another cheer *Cross-fade to full lighting on court*	(Page 15)
Cue 11	**Lucie** is helped to the door; clock ticks *The Lights change*	(Page 23)

Cue 12	**Carton** takes up a candle *Covering spot on candle*	(Page 26)
Cue 13	**Second Onlooker**: " ... the Stryver chambers ... " *Cross-fade to Stryver chambers lighting* *with fireglow effect*	(Page 27)
Cue 14	**Carton** stops *Light shines into his face*	(Page 29)
Cue 15	**Mr Lorry**: " ... wasted tears ... " *Cross-fade to wine shop lighting*	(Page 29)
Cue 16	**Dancers** scatter *Lights judder; then a light sweeps down* *across the audience*	(Page 29)
Cue 17	Screams and shouts *Light ends on back of coach with plunging horses effect*	(Page 29)
Cue 18	Crowd disperse *Lights focus on **Defarges** during following*	(Page 31)
Cue 19	**Defarges** listen *Lights go out on **Defarges***	(Page 32)
Cue 20	When ready *Lights come up again on Soho setting* *with dappled shade effect*	(Page 32)
Cue 21	**Lucie** moves to **Darnay** *Lights fade*	(Page 38)
Cue 22	**Postilion**: " — the setting sun." *Crimson light on **Marquis***	(Page 39)
Cue 23	**Marquis**: "It will die out — directly." *Crimson light goes out*	(Page 39)
Cue 24	**Narrators** withdraw *Lights dim slightly*	(Page 42)
Cue 25	**Defarge**: "We have not heard of it." *Lights focus on Soho setting*	(Page 46)
Cue 26	**Defarge** follows **Mme Defarge** off *Lights cross-fade to **Mr Lorry***	(Page 48)

A Tale of Two Cities

Cue 27	**Dr Manette** goes *Lights darken*	(Page 50)
Cue 28	Scene 16 begins *Lights change to "dark and stormy" effect during scene*	(Page 50)
Cue 29	Crackle of thunder *Light yellows, darkens*	(Page 52)
Cue 30	**First Narrator**: "... seven hundred and eighty-nine..." *Flash of lightning*	(Page 52)
Cue 31	**Mr Lorry**: "All safe and well..." *Bright flash of lightning*	(Page 53)
Cue 32	They fire off a round *Black-out*	(Page 53)

ACT II

To open: Dim light; covering spot on candle

Cue 33	**Carton** disappears from sight *Rush of flame effect, then shadowy lighting*	(Page 54)
Cue 34	**Defarge**: "But treasure of a kind!" *Lights go out on **Defarge***	(Page 56)
Cue 35	Music reaches crescendo *Light focuses on the three heads*	(Page 56)
Cue 36	**Red Caps** leave *Light goes tight in on **Gabelle***	(Page 58)
Cue 37	Scene 5 begins *Lights cross-fade to Lucie and Darnay*	(Page 59)
Cue 38	**Darnay** dashes away *Lights cross-fade to Place du Carrousel lighting*	(Page 60)
Cue 39	Guillotine moves back *Lights come down on main stage, remaining on higher level*	(Page 63)
Cue 40	**Mr Lorry**: "Save the prisoner Evrémonde at La Force!" *Lights down on **Dr Manette** on higher level*	(Page 64)

Cue 41	**Lorry** goes *Lights cross-fade to Tellson's Bank*	(Page 64)
Cue 42	Everyone exits apart from family group *Lights cross-fade to Dr Manette's apartment*	(Page 68)
Cue 43	**Dr Manette** turns and goes *Lights fade*	(Page 69)
Cue 44	A bell tolls *Street lamp light*	(Page 69)
Cue 45	Door clangs *Narrow shaft of light with prison bar pattern on* **Darnay**; *covering spot on* **Seamstress**'s *candle*	(Page 70)
Cue 46	Another door bangs **Darnay**'s *light and candle cover fade; fireglow comes up*	(Page 70)
Cue 47	**Mr Lorry**: "Good-night." *Lights cross-fade to Chemist's Shop*	(Page 74)
Cue 48	**Carton**: "I can't sleep." *Lights focus on* **Carton**	(Page 74)
Cue 49	**Carton** turns and walks away. A beat *Bright light*	(Page 75)
Cue 50	**Carton**: "Now, Mr Barsad ... " *Lights darken to prison gloom*	(Page 78)
Cue 51	**Gaoler**: 'Come, citizen. It is time." *Lights cross-fade to focus on* **Carton**	(Page 81)
Cue 452	**Carton**: " ... to the last." *Lights focus on* **Mr Lorry**	(Page 81)
Cue 53	**Mr Lorry**: " ... we are pursued by nothing else!" *Whirl of light, then lighting on* **Mme Defarge** *and* **Miss Pross**	(Page 82)
Cue 54	**Pross**: " ... never to be broken as long as my life lasts." *Lights cross-fade to focus on* **Carton**	(Page 83)
Cue 55	**Carton**: " ... I have ever known." *Light burns brighter and brighter*	(Page 84)

EFFECTS PLOT

ACT I

Cue 1	To open *Carriage wheels, creaks and rumbles; horses neigh, pant, gallop. Sudden braking; carriage skids and squeals to silence*	(Page 1)
Cue 2	**Sixth:** "He doesn't understand!!" *Crash of a great door — thunderous, clanging, deadly sound, with echo*	(Page 1)
Cue 3	Firelight *Distant sounds of the sea with pipe or fiddle playing*	(Page 2)
Cue 4	**Mr Lorry:** " ... great repute in Paris ... " *Music*	(Page 3)
Cue 5	**Dr Manette** watches the **Citizens** *Carriage approaches*	(Page 4)
Cue 6	Voice inside carriage cries: "Stop!" *Cut carriage noise*	(Page 5)
Cue 7	They enter the stable *Sound of horses moving, rustling straw, soft whinnying*	(Page 5)
Cue 8	Fierce interchange of blows *Sounds of horses neighing and stamping in their stalls*	(Page 7)
Cue 9	**Boy** staggers into **Dr Manette**'s arms *Music — distant, ominous*	(Page 7)
Cue 10	Lights fade *Music swells up*	(Page 7)
Cue 11	When ready *Music fades*	(Page 7)
Cue 12	The Lights change *Travelling music; shanty; seagulls; thundering wheels; single pipe plays on as other sounds fade*	(Page 8)

Cue 13	**Lucie:** "Thank God for this, thank God!" *Music rises*	(Page 12)
Cue 14	**Defarge:** "To the barrier!" *Hooves and wheels*	(Page 13)
Cue 15	**Lucie:** "... the great grove of stars ——" *Sounds of journey die away*	(Page 13)
Cue 16	**Carton:** "... suffered or done." *Carriage sound, continuing under dialogue*	(Page 13)
Cue 17	Jeers, boos *Thud of rotten tomato*	(Page 15)
Cue 18	Every eye is riveted on **Carton** and **Darnay** *Echo of distant music*	(Page 21)
Cue 19	All on stage look into audience *Clock ticking*	(Page 23)
Cue 20	**Voice:** "NOT GUILTY!!". Buzzing swells *Joyful music*	(Page 23)
Cue 21	**Carton** examines himself in the mirror *Sad, serious distant music*	(Page 26)
Cue 22	**Carton:** "... it may be a quarter of an hour later." *Bells sound the half-hour*	(Page 27)
Cue 23	**Second Onlooker:** "... the damp dark morning." *Bell tolls three*	(Page 27)
Cue 24	The room vanishes *Sad music*	(Page 29)
Cue 25	**Mr Lorry:** "... and it was gone. ..." *Music builds*	(Page 29)
Cue 26	During dance *Noise of great coach and pounding hooves, getting closer; then screeching of brakes, whinnying of horses*	(Page 29)
Cue 27	Lights focus on **Defarges** *Crowd's footsteps echo beneath dialogue*	(Page 31)

A Tale of Two Cities

Cue 28	**Mme Defarge**: "He shall be registered tomorrow." *Footsteps grow louder, echo, fade, grow, cross, recross — continuing under scene change*	(Page 32)
Cue 29	Opening of SCENE 11 *Birdsong; footsteps continue, fading during scene*	(Page 32)
Cue 30	**Darnay**: " ... deserve your confidence ——— " *Music, underscoring dialogue*	(Page 38)
Cue 31	**Dr Manette**: " ... your wedding day." *Music rises*	(Page 38)
Cue 32	Lights fade *Carriage wheels, pounding hooves, crack of whips*	(Page 38)
Cue 33	**Gabelle**: "Suddenly ———" *Hand scrabbling, fall of pebbles*	(Page 40)
Cue 34	**Marquis**: "Good." *Noise of a carriage*	(Page 40)
Cue 35	**Marquis** climbs the stairs *Elegant, sinister harpsichord tune*	(Page 42)
Cue 36	The **Marquis** falls *Wedding bells*	(Page 43)
Cue 37	**Second Narrator**: " — and who his father had been." *Music fades*	(Page 43)
Cue 38	**Mr Lorry**: " .. she was no unsuitable figure!" *Music; footsteps*	(Page 50)
Cue 39	**Lucie**: " .. her father's firm and equal." *Crackle of thunder*	(Page 52)
Cue 40	**First Narrator**: " ... seven hundred and eighty-nine ..." *Crack of thunder*	(Page 52)
Cue 41	**Lucie**: " ... all afternoon." *Crack of thunder; marching feet in the distance*	(Page 53)
Cue 42	**Mr Lorry**: " ... after my long day. " *Thunder*	(Page 53)
Cue 43	**Mr Lorry**: "All safe and well." *Mighty crack of thunder*	(Page 53)

ACT II

Cue 44	As Act II begins *Piano music; roar in background*	(Page 54)
Cue 45	**Carton**: " ... than I am to them ... ?" *Roar breaks through, very loud*	(Page 54)
Cue 46	Rush of flame effect *Smoke, alarm bells, drums*	(Page 54)
Cue 47	**Defarge** and the **Revolutionary** enter the cell *Noise reduces to deep, hoarse roar*	(Page 55)
Cue 48	**Three Citizens** advance *Rising music*	(Page 56)
Cue 49	Light focuses on three heads *Music stops*	(Page 56)
Cue 50	**Lucie** smiles and goes *Sinister restless music*	(Page 59)
Cue 451	Lights cross-fade to Place du Carrousel *Distant drumming, continuing under dialogue*	(Page 61)
Cue 52	The **Red Caps** propel **Darnay** away *Louder drumming, continuing under dialogue*	(Page 62)
Cue 53	**Lucie**: " ... whatever our fear." *Drumming gets louder*	(Page 62)
Cue 54	**Dr Manette** opens the windows *Sounds become intense*	(Page 63)
Cue 55	Execution takes place; cheer *Roll of drums*	(Page 63)
Cue 56	**Mme Defarge**: "TWO!" *Single drum beat*	(Page 63)
Cue 57	**Lucie** and **Pross** hug and smile. A moment of peace *Music, continuing through scene change*	(Page 65)
Cue 58	**Darnay** is lifted up *Jagged piece of the Marseillaise*	(Page 68)

A Tale of Two Cities   95

Cue 59   The Lights fade   (Page 69)
          Bell tolls

Cue 60   **Carton** and **Barsad** turn and go   (Page 70)
          Door clangs

Cue 61   **Darnay**: "... how could she be here?"   (Page 70)
          Clang of prison door; another door bangs

Cue 62   **Darnay** and the **Seamstress** vanish   (Page 70)
          Crackle of fire

Cue 63   **Chemist** withdraws   (Page 74)
          Carton's theme plays

Cue 64   Lights darken to prison gloom   (Page 78)
          Bell strikes

Cue 65   **First Narrator**: "... he never once thought of him ... " (Page 79)
          Bells toll

Cue 66   **Darnay**: "Will I be the first or last? ... "   (Page 79)
          Echoing footsteps; key in lock; door creaking

Cue 67   **Barsad**, the **Gaoler** and **Darnay** exit   (Page 81)
          Door crashes to; distant footsteps; bell tolls ten o'clock;
          after tenth stroke five doors clang open

Cue 68   Lights focus on **Mr Lorry**   (Page 82)
          Galloping horses, grinding wheels

Cue 69   **Miss Pross**: " ... faints or dies."   (Page 82)
          Flash; crash

Cue 70   Lights fade   (Page 83)
          Smoke

Cue 71   **Executioner**: " ... traitor to the people."   (Page 83)
          Sound of blade dropping

Cue 72   **Executioner**: " ... traitor to the people!"   (Page 83)
          Sound of blade dropping, then sound of wind blowing

Cue 73   **Carton**: " ... and wearing out."   (Page 83)
          Quiet music: Carton's theme

Cue 74   Lights snap out   (Page 84)
          Music rises to crescendo; sound of blade dropping,
          music cuts out sharply, leaving sound of cold wind